DEREK BLACK

# WINNERS AND LOSERS

## The Book of

# CANADIAN POLITICAL LISTS

ILLUSTRATIONS BY
**Tom Andres**

 **METHUEN**

Toronto     New York     London     Sydney     Auckland

This book is dedicated to two people: my father, Robert S. Black, and Mr. Fred Hostetter.

My father shortly before his death summed up his life by saying, "I've had a good life just being neighbourly." I believe this statement typifies both gentlemen.

Copyright © 1984 by Derek Black

**Canadian Cataloguing in Publication Data**

Black, Derek, 1935-
  Winners and losers

Previous ed. had title: Election Canada.
Bibliography: p.
ISBN 0-458-97640-7

1. Prime ministers—Canada.   2. Elections—Canada.
I. Title.   II. Title: Election Canada.

| | | |
|---|---|---|
| FC26.P7B53 1984 | 324.971 | C84-098439-1 |
| F1005.B53 1984 | | |

*40,345*

COVER & BOOK DESIGN: Brant Cowie/Artplus

Printed and bound in Canada

1  2  3  4      84      88  87  86  85

# Acknowledgments

When the idea for this book was first conceived, Stuart Fergusson had much to do with the original planning, inspiration, and research. A special thanks also goes to The Hon. Muriel Fergusson, senator, and Mr. Eric Spicer, parliamentary librarian, for their advice and encouragement. Many research books were opened with their kind assistance.

Edith Sullivan's many hours at the typewriter translating my handwriting also must not go unappreciated.

After several years of dormancy, the book finally reached its conclusion, and Mark Greenwood, David Cuthbertson, and Ian Eddy are to be thanked for their assistance in information gathering at this later date.

Donald Striffler must be thanked for his graphic design work. The maps in this book are primarily of his invention.

The help and patience of the staff at the Public Archives of Canada, Ottawa, and Mount Allison University, Sackville, New Brunswick, are also greatly appreciated.

I would like to acknowledge as well the fine job done by my editor, Susan Gaitskell.

Finally, but most importantly, I wish to thank my wife, Paula, for her support and assistance. Without her, this project never would have been finished. I thank her for believing in me and my work.

# Preface

*Winners and Losers* is a guide to elections in Canada and those men and women who participated in them.

I first became interested in this project after having asked many of my fellow Canadians, "Who was the first prime minister of Canada?" When I found many could not tell me, I resolved to compile an easy reference source of Canadian political events. I have tried to develop a book which may be used by students to supplement their Canadian history texts or by average citizens to settle an argument on election eve.

Regardless of our party affiliations, we should be aware that Sir John A. Macdonald was the founding father of our country and that Mackenzie King guided us through the turbulant 1920s, 30s and 40s.

All holders of public office had to have some greatness in them; otherwise they could not have risen above the mainstream, and it is the intention of this book not just to honour them, but to give us all a little better understanding of who they were, and what they accomplished.

It is my hope that all the information in this book is correct. However, it is possible that errors have slipped through unnoticed. In subsequent editions, published in future election years, I hope these errors will be removed. If you, the reader, spot an error or omission, please do not hesitate to notify the publisher.

It is my sincere wish, however majestic, to make this book the bible of Canadian politics for every Canadian. I want us all to be more knowledgeable of our political heritage and to be more appreciative of those who have held political office in Canada.

DEREK BLACK

# Contents

# ONE

# Mr. Prime Minister

A picture is worth a thousand words. Tom Andres' caricatures and the capsule biographies are intended to give the reader a quick overview of the lives of the prime ministers.

1st PRIME MINISTER

# Sir John Alexander Macdonald

BORN  January 11, 1815

BIRTHPLACE  Glasgow, Scotland

EDUCATION  Royal Grammar School (Kingston)

FAMILY LINEAGE  Scottish

RELIGION  Presbyterian

PARENTS  Hugh Macdonald  Helen Shaw

FATHER'S OCCUPATION  Merchant

WIVES  Isabelle Clark (1843) Susan Agnes Bernard (1867)

CHILDREN  3

PROFESSION  Lawyer

POLITICAL PARTY  Conservative

PROVINCE REPRESENTED  Ontario (Upper Canada)

PUBLICATIONS  None

MILITARY SERVICE  None

TERM OF OFFICE  1867-73, 1878-91

AGE WHEN TAKING OFFICE  52

CABINET POSITIONS HELD
  Minister of justice and attorney general (1867-73)
  Minister of interior (1878-83)
  Minister of railways and canals (1889-91)

APPOINTED TO PRIVY COUNCIL   1867

APPOINTED TO IMPERIAL PRIVY COUNCIL   1872

HONORIFIC TITLES
   Knight Commander of the Order of the Bath (1867)
   Knight Grand Cross of the Order of the Bath (1884)

OCCUPATION AFTER OFFICE   Died in office

DATE OF DEATH   June 6, 1891

PLACE OF DEATH   Ottawa, Ontario

AGE AT DEATH   76

IMPORTANT CAREER EVENTS
   1836-Admitted to the bar of Upper Canada
   1844-First election to Upper Canada Legislature
   1854-Appointed attorney general
   1864-Delegate to Charlottetown and Québec conferences
   1866-Chairman, London conference
   1867-Appointed first prime minister of Canada
         First elected to House of Commons (Kingston, Ont.)
   1872-Re-elected
   1873-Resigns as prime minister
   1874-Re-elected to house (unseated by petition)
         Re-elected (by-election)
   1878-Defeated (Kingston, Ont.); re-elected (Marquette, Man.)
   1878-91 Prime minister
         Re-elected (Victoria, B.C.*)
   1882-Re-elected (Carleton, Ont. and Lennox, Ont.†)
   1887-Re-elected (Kingston, Ont. and Carleton, Ont.†)
   1891-Re-elected (Kingston, Ont.)
         Died in office

*Re-elected after becoming prime minister.      †Resigned seat.

2nd PRIME MINISTER

# Alexander Mackenzie

BORN   January 28, 1822

BIRTHPLACE   Dunkeld, Scotland

EDUCATION   Public schools at Moulin, Dunkeld, and Perth, Scotland

FAMILY LINEAGE   Scottish

RELIGION   Baptist

PARENTS   Alexander Mackenzie
Mary Fleming

FATHER'S OCCUPATION   Builder

WIVES   Helen Neil
Jane Sym (1853)

CHILDREN   3

PROFESSION   Contractor

POLITICAL PARTY   Liberal

PROVINCE REPRESENTED   Ontario (Upper Canada)

PUBLICATIONS   *Speeches in Scotland and Canada* (1876)
*The Life and Speeches of George Brown* (1882)

MILITARY SERVICE   Major, Twenty-seventh Lambton Battalion Volunteer Infantry (1866-74)

TERM OF OFFICE 1873-78

AGE WHEN TAKING OFFICE 51

CABINET POSITION HELD
  Minister of public works (1873-78)

APPOINTED TO PRIVY COUNCIL 1873

HONORIFIC TITLES None*

OCCUPATION AFTER OFFICE Died as member of Parliament

DATE OF DEATH April 17, 1892

PLACE OF DEATH Toronto, Ontario

AGE AT DEATH 70

IMPORTANT CAREER EVENTS
  1861-Elected to Legislative Assembly of Canada
  1867-First elected to House of Commons (Lambton, Ont.)
  1872-Re-elected to House of Commons (Lambton, Ont.)
  1873-Leader of Liberal party
  1873-78-Prime minister
  1873-Re-elected to House in by-election†
  1874-78-Re-elected to House
  1878-Defeated as prime minister
  1882-Re-elected to House of Commons (York East, Ont.)
  1887-91-Re-elected to House (York East, Ont.)
  1892-Died while still a member of Parliament

*Only prime minister of the first eight to refuse knighthood.
†Re-elected after becoming prime minister.

3rd PRIME MINISTER

# Sir John Joseph Caldwell Abbott

BORN  March 12, 1821

BIRTHPLACE  St. Andrews, Québec (Lower Canada)

EDUCATION  University of McGill (B.C.L.)

FAMILY LINEAGE  English

RELIGION  Anglican

PARENTS  Joseph Abbott
         Harriett Bradford

FATHER'S OCCUPATION  Minister

WIFE  Mary Bethune (1849)

CHILDREN  None

PROFESSION  Lawyer

POLITICAL PARTY  Conservative

PROVINCE REPRESENTED  Québec

PUBLICATIONS  None

MILITARY SERVICE  Commanded Argenteuil Rangers (1866)

TERM OF OFFICE  1891-92

AGE WHEN TAKING OFFICE  70

CABINET POSITION HELD
   Minister without portfolio (1887-91)

APPOINTED TO PRIVY COUNCIL    1887

HONORIFIC TITLE    Knight Commander of the Order of the Bath (1892)

OCCUPATION AFTER OFFICE    Died eleven months after leaving office

DATE OF DEATH    October 30, 1893

PLACE OF DEATH    Montréal, Québec

AGE AT DEATH    72

IMPORTANT CAREER EVENTS

1847-Called to Quebec bar
1855-80-Dean of Faculty of Law, McGill University
1857-Elected to Legislative Assembly (Québec)
1867-First Elected to House of Commons (Argenteuil, Qué.)
1872-74-Re-elected (unseated by petition)
1878-Defeated (Argenteuil, Qué.)
1880-Elected in by-election (election voided)
1881-Elected in by-election (Argenteuil, Qué.)
1882-Re-elected
1887-Appointed to Senate (government leader in Senate)
1887-88-Mayor of Montréal
1891-Prime minister (June 16)
1892-Resigned office of prime minister (Dec. 5)

4th PRIME MINISTER

# Sir John Sparrow David Thompson

BORN   November 10, 1844

BIRTHPLACE   Halifax, Nova Scotia

EDUCATION   Halifax Common School
            Free Church Academy

FAMILY LINEAGE   Irish

RELIGION   Catholic

PARENTS   John Sparrow Thompson
          Charlotte Pottinger

FATHER'S OCCUPATION   Civil servant

WIFE   Annie E. Affleck (1870)

CHILDREN   5

PROFESSION   Lawyer

POLITICAL PARTY   Conservative

PROVINCE REPRESENTED   Nova Scotia

PUBLICATIONS   None

MILITARY SERVICE   None

TERM OF OFFICE   1892-94

AGE WHEN TAKING OFFICE   48

CABINET POSITION HELD   Minister of justice and attorney general (1885-94)

APPOINTED TO PRIVY COUNCIL   1885

APPOINTED TO IMPERIAL PRIVY COUNCIL   1894

HONORIFIC TITLE   Knight Commander of the Order of the Bath (1888)

OCCUPATION AFTER OFFICE   Died in office

DATE OF DEATH   December 12, 1894

PLACE OF DEATH   Windsor Castle, England

AGE AT DEATH   50

IMPORTANT CAREER EVENTS
    1865-Called to Nova Scotia bar
    1877-Elected to Legislative Assembly of Nova Scotia
    1878-82-Attorney General of Nova Scotia
    1882-Premier of Nova Scotia
    1885-First elected to House of Commons* (by-election for
        Antigonish, Nova Scotia)
    1887-91-Re-elected
    1894-Prime minister (Dec. 5)
    1894-Died in office†

*After accepting cabinet position.
†After accepting membership to Imperial Privy Council.

5th PRIME MINISTER

# Sir Mackenzie Bowell

BORN   December 27, 1823

BIRTHPLACE   Rickinghall, Suffolk, England

EDUCATION   Printer's apprentice

FAMILY LINEAGE   English

FATHER   John Bowell

FATHER'S OCCUPATION   Contractor

WIFE   Harriet Louise Moore (1847)

CHILDREN   9

RELIGION   Methodist

PROFESSION   Printer and editor (*The Intelligencer*)

POLITICAL PARTY   Conservative

PROVINCE REPRESENTED   Ontario

PUBLICATIONS   None

MILITARY SERVICE   Major, Forty-ninth Hastings Battalion of Militia (1867-72)

TERM OF OFFICE   1894-96

AGE WHEN TAKING OFFICE   70

CABINET POSITIONS HELD
Minister of customs ( 1878-92 )
Minister of militia ( 1892 )
Minister of trade and commerce ( 1892-94 )

APPOINTED TO PRIVY COUNCIL 1878

HONORIFIC TITLE Knight Commander of the Order of the Bath
( 1895 )

OCCUPATION AFTER OFFICE Senator

DATE OF DEATH December 10, 1917

PLACE OF DEATH Belleville, Ontario

AGE AT DEATH 93

IMPORTANT CAREER EVENTS
1867-First elected to House of Commons (North Hastings, Ont.)
1872, 74, 78-Re-elected
1878-Re-elected in by-election*
1882, 87, 91-Re-elected
1892-Appointed to Senate
1894-Prime minister (Dec. 21)
1896-Resigned office of prime minister (Apr. 27)

*Re-elected after accepting cabinet position.

6th PRIME MINISTER

# Sir Charles Hibbert Tupper, Bart.

BORN  July 2, 1821

BIRTHPLACE  Amherst, Nova Scotia

EDUCATION  Horton Academy
             Edinburgh University (M.D.)

FAMILY LINEAGE  English

RELIGION  Baptist

PARENTS  Rev. Charles Tupper
           Miriam Lockhart Low

FATHER'S OCCUPATION  Minister

WIFE  Frances Amelia Morse (1846)

CHILDREN  6

PROFESSION  Physician

POLITICAL PARTY  Conservative

PROVINCE REPRESENTED  Nova Scotia

PUBLICATIONS  *Recollections of Sixty Years* (1914)

MILITARY SERVICE  None

TERM OF OFFICE  May-July 1896

AGE WHEN TAKING OFFICE  74

CABINET POSITIONS HELD

Minister of inland revenue (1872-73)
Minister of customs (1873)
Minister of public works (1878-79)
Minister of railways and canals (1879-84)
Minister of finance (1887-88)
Secretary of state (1896)

APPOINTED TO PRIVY COUNCIL   1870

APPOINTED TO IMPERIAL PRIVY COUNCIL   1907

HONORIFIC TITLES   Companion of the Order of the Bath (1867)
Knight Commander of the Order of the Bath (1879)
Knight Grand Cross of the Order of St. Michael and St. George (1886)
Baronet of the United Kingdom (1888)

OCCUPATION AFTER OFFICE   Member of Parliament

DATE OF DEATH   October 30, 1915

PLACE OF DEATH   Bexley Heath, Kent, England

AGE AT DEATH   93

IMPORTANT CAREER EVENTS

1855-Elected to Legislative Assembly of Nova Scotia
1864-67-Premier of Nova Scotia
Delegate to Charlottetown, Québec, and London conferences
1867-First president of Canadian Medical Association
Elected to House of Commons (Cumberland, Nova Scotia)

1870-Re-elected in by-election*
1872, 74, 78-Re-elected
1878-Re-elected in by-election*
1882-Re-elected (resigned 1884)
1884-87-High commissioner to England
1887-Re-elected (re-election after election declared void)
1889-96-High commissioner to England (resigns Commons
    seat)
1896-Prime minister (May 1-July 8)†
    Re-elected
    Leader of the opposition (1896-1901)
1900-Lost general election

*Re-elected after accepting cabinet position.
†Shortest term as prime minister.

7th PRIME MINISTER

# Sir Wilfrid Laurier

BORN  November 20, 1841

BIRTHPLACE  St. Lin, Québec (Lower Canada)

EDUCATION  L'Assomption College
McGill University (B.C.L.)

FAMILY LINEAGE  French

RELIGION  Catholic

PARENTS  Carolus Laurier  Marcelle Martineau

FATHER'S OCCUPATION  Land surveyor

WIFE  Zoë Lafontaine

CHILDREN  None

PROFESSION  Lawyer

POLITICAL PARTY  Liberal

PROVINCE REPRESENTED  Québec

PUBLICATIONS  *Lectures on Political Liberalism* (1877)

MILITARY SERVICE  None

TERM OF OFFICE  1896-1911

AGE WHEN TAKING OFFICE  54

CABINET POSITION HELD
Minister of inland revenue-1877-78

APPOINTED TO PRIVY COUNCIL  1877

APPOINTED TO IMPERIAL PRIVY COUNCIL  1897

HONORIFIC TITLE  Knight Commander of the Order of the Bath
(1897)

OCCUPATION AFTER OFFICE  Member of Parliament

DATE OF DEATH  February 17, 1919

PLACE OF DEATH  Ottawa, Ontario

AGE AT DEATH  77

IMPORTANT CAREER EVENTS
    1865-Called to Québec bar
    1871-Elected to Legislative Assembly of Québec
    1874-First elected to House of Commons (Drummond-
        Arthabaska, Qué.)
    1877-Defeated in by-election* (re-elected in by-election-
        Québec East)
    1878, 82, 87, 91-Re-elected
    1887-96 Leader of the opposition (party leader 1887-1919)
    1896-Re-elected (Québec East and Saskatchewan,
        N.W.T.**)*
    1896-1911-Prime minister
    1896-Re-elected in by-election†
    1900-Re-elected
    1904-Re-elected (Québec East and Wright, Qué.**)*
    1908-Re-elected (Québec East and Ottawa, Ont.**)*
    1911-Re-elected (Québec East and Soulonges**)*
    1917-Re-elected (Québec East), defeated (Ottawa, Ont.)
    1919-Died while still a member of Parliament

*Re-elected after accepting cabinet position.      **Resigned seat.
†Re-elected after assuming office of prime minister.

8th PRIME MINISTER

# Sir Robert Laird Borden

BORN  June 26, 1854

BIRTHPLACE  Grand Pré, Nova Scotia

EDUCATION  Acadia Villa Seminary, Horton, Nova Scotia

FAMILY LINEAGE  English

RELIGION  Anglican

PARENTS  Andrew Borden
Eunice Laird

FATHER'S OCCUPATION  Farmer

WIFE  Laura Bond (1889)

CHILDREN  None

PROFESSION  Lawyer

POLITICAL PARTY  Conservative

PROVINCE REPRESENTED  Nova Scotia

PUBLICATIONS  *Canadian Constitutional Studies* (1922)
*Canada in the Commonwealth* (1929)
*Robert Laird Borden: His Memoirs* (1938, published posthumously by nephew)

MILITARY SERVICE  None

TERM OF OFFICE  1911-1920

AGE WHEN TAKING OFFICE   57

CABINET POSITION HELD
   Secretary of state for external affairs (1912-1920)

APPOINTED TO PRIVY COUNCIL   1911

APPOINTED TO IMPERIAL PRIVY COUNCIL   1912

HONORIFIC TITLE   Knight Grand Cross of the Order of St. Michael and St. George (1914)

OCCUPATION AFTER OFFICE   Director of numerous companies
                         Chancellor of Queen's University
                         (1924-30)

DATE OF DEATH   June 10, 1937

PLACE OF DEATH   Ottawa, Ontario

AGE AT DEATH   82

IMPORTANT CAREER EVENTS
   1878-Called to Nova Scotia bar
   1896-First elected to House of Commons (Halifax, N.S.)
   1900-Re-elected
   1901-20-Conservative party leader
   1904-Defeated
   1905-Re-elected at by-election (Carleton, Ont.)
   1908-Re-elected (Carleton, Ont.*; Halifax, N.S.)
   1911-17-Re-elected (Halifax and Kings, N.S.*)
   1911-20-Prime minister
   1911-Re-elected (Halifax, N.S.†)
   1920-Resigned as prime minister

*Resigned seat.
†Re-elected after assuming office of prime minister.

9th PRIME MINISTER

# Arthur Meighen

BORN  June 16, 1874

BIRTHPLACE  Anderson, Ontario

EDUCATION  St. Mary's Collegiate
University of Toronto (B.A.)

FAMILY LINEAGE  Irish

RELIGION  Presbyterian

PARENTS  Joseph Meighen  Mary Jane Bell

FATHER'S OCCUPATION  Farmer

WIFE  Jessie Isabel Cox (1904)

CHILDREN  3

PROFESSION  Lawyer

POLITICAL PARTY  Conservative

PROVINCE REPRESENTED  Ontario

PUBLICATIONS  *Overseas Addresses* (1921)
*The Greatest Englishman in History* (1836)
*Unrevised and Unrepented: Debating Speeches and Others* (1949)

MILITARY SERVICE  None

TERM OF OFFICE  1920-21, 1926

AGE WHEN TAKING OFFICE  46

CABINET POSITIONS HELD
  Solicitor general (1913)
  Secretary of state (1917)
  Minister of the interior
    (1917)
Minister of mines (1919)
Secretary of state for external
  affairs (1920-21, 1926)
Minister without portfolio
  (1932-35)

APPOINTED TO PRIVY COUNCIL   1915

APPOINTED TO IMPERIAL PRIVY COUNCIL   1920

HONORIFIC TITLES   None

OCCUPATION AFTER OFFICE   Member of Parliament and senator
                         (1932)

DATE OF DEATH   August 5, 1960

PLACE OF DEATH   Toronto, Ontario

AGE AT DEATH   86

IMPORTANT CAREER EVENTS
  1902-Called to Manitoba bar
  1908-First elected to House of Commons (Portage la Prairie)
  1911-Re-elected
  1913-Re-elected in by-election*
  1917-Re-elected
  1920-21-Prime minister
  1920-26-Conservative party leader
  1921-Defeated
  1922-Re-elected at by-election (Grenville, Ont.)
  1925-Re-elected (Portage la Prairie, Man.)
  1926-Prime minister (June 29-Sept. 25); defeated
  1932-42-Member of Senate
  1941-42-Party leader
  1942-Defeated in by-election (York South, Ont.)

*Re-elected after accepting cabinet position.

10th PRIME MINISTER

# William Lyon Mackenzie King

BORN  December 17, 1874

BIRTHPLACE  Kitchener (Berlin), Ontario

EDUCATION  University of Toronto (B.A., L.L.B.)
University of Chicago
Harvard University (M.A., Ph.D.)

FAMILY LINEAGE  Scottish

RELIGION  Presbyterian

PARENTS  John King
Isabel Grace Mackenzie

FATHER'S OCCUPATION  Lawyer

WIFE  None

CHILDREN  None

PROFESSION  Civil servant

POLITICAL PARTY  Liberal

PROVINCE REPRESENTED  Ontario

PUBLICATIONS  *The Secret of Heroism* (1906)
*Industry and Humanity* (1918)
*The Message of the Carillon and other Addresses* (1927)
*Canada at Britain's Side* (1941)
*Canada and the Fight for Freedom* (1944)

MILITARY SERVICE  None

TERM OF OFFICE  1921-26, 1926-30, 1935-48

AGE WHEN TAKING OFFICE  47

CABINET POSITIONS HELD
Minister of labour (1901-11)
Secretary of state for external affairs (1921-26, 1935-46)

APPOINTED TO PRIVY COUNCIL  1909

APPOINTED TO IMPERIAL PRIVY COUNCIL  1922

HONORIFIC TITLES  None

OCCUPATION AFTER OFFICE  Member of Parliament

DATE OF DEATH  July 22, 1950

PLACE OF DEATH  Kingsmere, Québec

AGE AT DEATH  75

IMPORTANT CAREER EVENTS
1900-Deputy minister of labour
1908-First elected to House of Commons (Waterloo North,
    Ont.)
1909-Re-elected in by-election†
1911-Defeated
1917-Defeated (York North, Ont.)
1919-Re-elected in by-election (Prince, P.E.I.)
1919-48-Liberal party leader
1921-Re-elected (York North, Ont.)*
1921-26-Prime minister
1922-Re-elected in by-election (Jan. 19)*
1925-Defeated
1926-Re-elected in by-election (Prince Albert, Sask.)

Re-elected
Re-elected in by-election*
1926-30-Prime minister
1930-35, 40-Re-elected
1935-48-Prime minister
1945-Defeated; re-elected in by-election (Glengarry, Ont.)
1948-Resigned as prime minister

*Re-elected after assuming office of prime minister.
†Re-elected after accepting cabinet position.

11th PRIME MINISTER

# Richard Bedford Bennett, first Viscount

BORN  July 3, 1870

BIRTHPLACE  Hopewell, New Brunswick

EDUCATION  Provincial Normal School, Fredericton, N.B.
Dalhousie University (L.L.B.)

FAMILY LINEAGE  English

RELIGION  Methodist

PARENTS  Henry John Bennett  Henrietta Stiles

FATHER'S OCCUPATION  Shipbuilder

WIFE  None

CHILDREN  None

PROFESSION  Lawyer

POLITICAL PARTY  Conservative

PROVINCE REPRESENTED  Alberta

PUBLICATIONS  None

MILITARY SERVICE  None

TERM OF OFFICE  1930-35

AGE WHEN TAKING OFFICE  60

CABINET POSITIONS HELD
Minister of justice (1921)

Minister of finance (1926)
Acting minister of the interior (1926)
Minister of mines (1926)
Secretary of state for external affairs (1930-35)

APPOINTED TO PRIVY COUNCIL   1921

APPOINTED TO IMPERIAL PRIVY COUNCIL   1930

HONORIFIC TITLE   Viscount of Mickleham, Calgary, and Hopewell

OCCUPATION AFTER OFFICE   Member of House of Lords

DATE OF DEATH   June 26, 1947

PLACE OF DEATH   Mickleham, England

AGE AT DEATH   76

IMPORTANT CAREER EVENTS
  1898-Elected to Assembly of Northwest Territories
  1900-Defeated in federal election (Calgary, Alta.)
  1909-Elected to Legislative Assembly of Alberta
  1911-First elected to House (Calgary, Alta.)
  1921-Defeated (Calgary West, Alta.)
  1925, 26, 30, 35-Re-elected
  1927-38-Conservative party leader
  1930-35-Prime minister
  1930-Re-elected in by-election (Calgary South, Alta.)*
  1935-38-Leader of opposition
  1938-Resigned from government
  1941-Created Viscount of Mickleham, Calgary, and Hopewell

*Last prime minister to seek re-election after assuming office.

12th PRIME MINISTER

# Louis Stephen St. Laurent

BORN   February 1, 1882

BIRTHPLACE   Compton, Québec

EDUCATION   St. Charles Seminary, Sherbrooke, Québec
Laval University (B.A., LL.L.)

FAMILY LINEAGE   French

RELIGION   Catholic

PARENTS   Jean-Baptiste Moise St. Laurent
Mary Broderick

FATHER'S OCCUPATION   Merchant

WIFE   Jeanne Renault (1908)

CHILDREN   5

PROFESSION   Lawyer

POLITICAL PARTY   Liberal

PROVINCE REPRESENTED   Québec

PUBLICATIONS   None

MILITARY SERVICE   None

TERM OF OFFICE   1948-57

AGE WHEN TAKING OFFICE   66

CABINET POSITIONS HELD
>Minister of justice and attorney general (1941-46)
>Secretary of state for external affairs (1946-48)
>Minister of justice (1948)

APPOINTED TO PRIVY COUNCIL   1941

APPOINTED TO IMPERIAL PRIVY COUNCIL   1946

HONORIFIC TITLES   None

OCCUPATION AFTER OFFICE   Lawyer

DATE OF DEATH   July 25, 1973

PLACE OF DEATH   Québec City

AGE AT DEATH   91

IMPORTANT CAREER EVENTS
>1905-Called to Québec bar
>1930-32-President of Canadian Bar Association
>1942-First elected to House of Commons in by-election
>>(Québec East, Qué.)
>1945, 49, 53, 57-Re-elected
>1948-Liberal party leader
>1948-57-Prime minister
>1957-Resigned as party leader

13th PRIME MINISTER

# John George Diefenbaker

BORN   September 18, 1895

BIRTHPLACE   Neustadt, Ontario

EDUCATION   University of Saskatchewan (B.A., M.A., L.L.B.)

FAMILY LINEAGE   German

RELIGION   Baptist

PARENTS   William Thomas Diefenbaker
Mary Florence Bannerman

FATHER'S OCCUPATION   Civil servant

WIVES   Edna Mae Brower (1929)
Olive Evangeline Palmer (1953)

CHILDREN   None

PROFESSION   Lawyer

POLITICAL PARTY   Conservative

PROVINCE REPRESENTED   Saskatchewan

PUBLICATIONS   One Canada: The Crusading Years, 1895-1956 (1975)
One Canada: The Years of Achievement, 1956-1962 (1976)
One Canada: The Tumultuous Years, 1962-1967 (1977)

MILITARY SERVICE   Lieutenant (World War I)

TERM OF OFFICE   1957-63

AGE WHEN TAKING OFFICE   61

CABINET POSITION HELD
   Secretary of state for external affairs (1957)

APPOINTED TO PRIVY COUNCIL   1957

APPOINTED TO IMPERIAL PRIVY COUNCIL   1957

HONORIFIC TITLES   None

OCCUPATION AFTER OFFICE   Member of Parliament

DATE OF DEATH   August 16, 1979

PLACE OF DEATH   Ottawa, Ontario

AGE AT DEATH   83

IMPORTANT CAREER EVENTS
   1914-17-Served overseas during World War I
   1919-Called to Saskatchewan bar
   1925, 26-Defeated in federal elections (Prince Albert, Sask.)
   1936-Leader of Saskatchewan Conservative party
   1940-First elected to House of Commons (Lake Centre, Sask.)
   1945, 49-Re-elected
   1953-Re-elected (Prince Albert, Sask.)
   1956-Chosen leader of federal Conservative party
   1957-63-Prime minister
   1957, 58, 62, 63, 65, 68, 72, 74, 79 Re-elected
   1979-Died while still a member of Parliament

14th PRIME MINISTER

# Lester Bowles Pearson

BORN   April 23, 1897

BIRTHPLACE   Newtonbrook, Ontario

EDUCATION   University of Toronto (B.A.)
Oxford University (M.A.)

FAMILY LINEAGE   Irish

RELIGION   Methodist

PARENTS   Edwin Arthur Pearson
Annie Sarah Bowles

FATHER'S OCCUPATION   Minister

WIFE   Maryon Elspeth Moody (1925)

CHILDREN   2

PROFESSION   Professor, civil servant

POLITICAL PARTY   Liberal

PROVINCE REPRESENTED   Ontario

PUBLICATIONS   *Democracy in World Politics* (1955)
*Diplomacy in the Nuclear Age* (1959)
*Mike-Vol. 1* (1972)
*Mike-Vol. 2* (1973)
*Mike-Vol. 3* (1975, published posthumously)

MILITARY SERVICE   Private, lieutenant, and flying officer (1915-18)

TERM OF OFFICE   1963-68

AGE WHEN TAKING OFFICE   65

CABINET POSITION HELD
   Secretary of state for external affairs (1948-57)

APPOINTED TO PRIVY COUNCIL   1948

APPOINTED TO IMPERIAL PRIVY COUNCIL   1963

HONORIFIC TITLES   None

OCCUPATION AFTER OFFICE   Author

DATE OF DEATH   December 27, 1972

PLACE OF DEATH   Ottawa, Ontario

AGE AT DEATH   75

IMPORTANT CAREER EVENTS
   1915-18-Served overseas during World War I
   1945-Ambassador to United States
   1946-Appointed under secretary for external affairs
   1948-First elected to House of Commons (by-election, Algoma East, Ont.)
   1949, 53, 57, 58, 62, 63, 65-Re-elected
   1951-52-President of United Nations General Assembly
   1957-Awarded Nobel Peace Prize
   1957-68-Leader of Liberal party
   1963-68-Prime minister
   1969-Resigned as prime minister

15th PRIME MINISTER

# Pierre Elliott Trudeau

BORN  October 18, 1919

BIRTHPLACE  Montréal, Québec

EDUCATION  Jean de Brébeuf College (B.A.)
University of Montréal (L.L.B.)
Harvard University (M.A.)
Ecole des Sciences Politiques, Paris
London School of Economics

FAMILY LINEAGE  French

RELIGION  Catholic

PARENTS  Charles-Emile Trudeau
Grace Elliott

FATHER'S OCCUPATION  Lawyer

WIFE  Margaret Sinclair (1971)

CHILDREN  3

PROFESSION  Lawyer

POLITICAL PARTY  Liberal

PROVINCE REPRESENTED  Québec

PUBLICATIONS  *La Grève de l'amiante* (1956)
*Deux innocents en Chine-rouge* (1961)
*The Future of Canadian Federalism* (1965)

> Politics: Canada (1966)
> Réponses (1967)
> Federalism and the French Canadians (1968)
> Les Cheminements de la politique (1970)
> Conversations with Canadians (1972)

MILITARY SERVICE   None

TERM OF OFFICE   1968-79, 1980-84

AGE WHEN TAKING OFFICE   48

CABINET POSITION HELD
   Minister of justice and attorney general (1967)

APPOINTED TO PRIVY COUNCIL   1967

HONORIFIC TITLES   None

IMPORTANT CAREER EVENTS
   1943-Called to Québec bar
   1949-Advisor to Privy Council
   1965-First elected to House of Commons (Mount Royal, Qué.)
   1968-Chosen leader of Liberal party
   1968-79-Prime minister
   1968, 72, 74, 79, 80-Re-elected
   1979-80-Leader of opposition
   1980-84-Prime minister

16th PRIME MINISTER

# Charles Joseph Clark

BORN  June 5, 1939

BIRTHPLACE  High River, Alberta

EDUCATION  University of Alberta (B.A., M.A.)
Dalhousie University

FAMILY LINEAGE  Scottish

RELIGION  Catholic

PARENTS  Charles A. Clark
Grace R. Welch

FATHER'S OCCUPATION  Publisher

WIFE  Maureen Anne McTeer

CHILD  1

PROFESSION  Journalist, lecturer

POLITICAL PARTY  Conservative

PROVINCE REPRESENTED  Alberta

PUBLICATIONS  None

MILITARY SERVICE  None

TERM OF OFFICE  1979-80

AGE WHEN TAKING OFFICE  39

CABINET POSITIONS HELD  None

APPOINTED TO PRIVY COUNCIL    1979

HONORIFIC TITLES    None

OCCUPATION AFTER OFFICE    Member of Parliament

IMPORTANT CAREER EVENTS

- 1963-65-National president of Conservative Student Federation
- 1964-Founding chairman of Canadian Political Youth Council
- 1972-First elected to House of Commons (Yellowhead, Alta.)
- 1974, 79, 80-Re-elected
- 1976-Leader of Conservative party and opposition leader
- 1979-80-Prime minister
- 1980-83-Leader of opposition
- 1983-Defeated as Conservative party leader by Brian Mulroney

# TWO

# Election Maps

The following section illustrates how the provinces voted in every federal election from 1867 to the present. Prime ministers – past, present and future – and party leaders who ran for Parliament in those elections are noted.

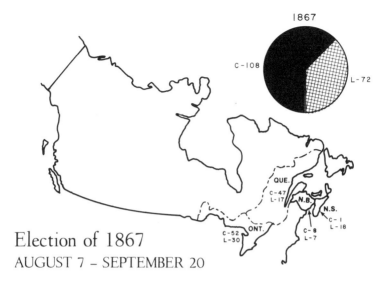

# Election of 1867
## AUGUST 7 – SEPTEMBER 20

**PRIME MINISTERS (PRESENT AND FUTURE)**

Macdonald-Kingston, Ont. (E)
Mackenzie-Lambton, Ont. (E)
Abbott-Argenteuil, Qué. (E)
Bowell-Hastings North, Ont. (E)
Tupper-Cumberland, N.S. (E)
(E)-Elected.

**PARTY LEADERS**

Sir John A. Macdonald-Conservative
George Brown-Liberal (unofficial)

**PROVINCIAL GOVERNMENTS AT TIME OF ELECTION**

N.B.-Conservative
N.S.-Conservative
P.E.I.-Unionist
Qué.-Conservative

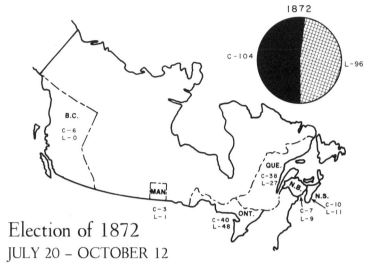

# Election of 1872
## JULY 20 – OCTOBER 12

**PRIME MINISTERS (PAST, PRESENT, AND FUTURE)**

Macdonald-Kingston, Ont. (E)
Mackenzie-Lambton, Ont. (E)
Abbott-Argenteuil, Qué. (E)
Bowell-Hastings North, Ont. (E)
Tupper-Cumberland, N.S. (E)
(E)-Elected.

**PARTY LEADERS**

Sir John A. Macdonald-Conservative
Sir Alexander Mackenzie-Liberal (unofficial)

**PROVINCIAL GOVERNMENTS AT TIME OF ELECTION**

| | |
|---|---|
| N.B.-Conservative | Qué.-Conservative |
| N.S.-Liberal | Man.-Conservative |
| Ont.-Unionist | B.C.-No federal affiliation |

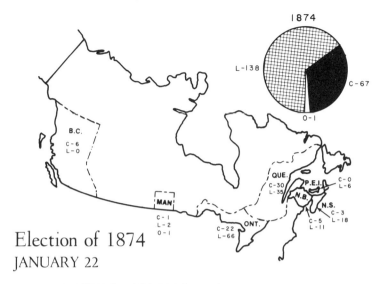

# Election of 1874
JANUARY 22

## PRIME MINISTERS (PAST, PRESENT, AND FUTURE)

Macdonald-Kingston, Ont. (E)
Mackenzie-Lambton, Ont. (E)
Abbott-Argenteuil, Qué. (E)
Bowell-Hastings North, Ont. (E)
Tupper-Cumberland, N.S. (E)
Laurier-Drummond-Arthabaska, Qué. (E)
(E)-Elected.

## PARTY LEADERS

Sir Alexander Mackenzie-Liberal
Sir John A. Macdonald-Conservative

## PROVINCIAL GOVERNMENTS AT TIME OF ELECTION

N.B.-Conservative                    Man.-Conservative
N.S.-Liberal                         B.C.-No federal affiliation
Ont.-Liberal                         P.E.I.-Conservative
Qué.-Conservative

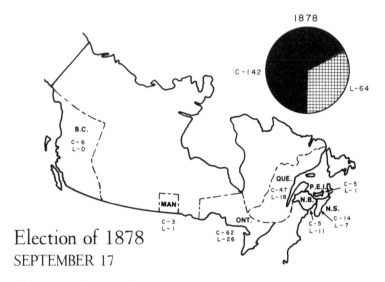

# Election of 1878
SEPTEMBER 17

## PRIME MINISTERS (PAST, PRESENT, AND FUTURE)

Macdonald-Kingston, Ont. (D), Marquette, Man. (E)
Mackenzie-Lambton, Ont. (E)
Abbott-Argenteuil, Qué. (D)*
Bowell-Hastings North, Ont. (E)
Tupper-Cumberland, N.S. (E)
Laurier-Québec East, Qué. (E)
(E)-Elected; (D) Defeated.
*Re-elected in by-election, Feb. 12, 1880.

## PARTY LEADERS

Sir John A. Macdonald-Conservative
Sir Alexander Mackenzie-Liberal

## PROVINCIAL GOVERNMENTS AT TIME OF ELECTION

N.B.-Conservative
N.S.-Liberal
Ont.-Liberal
Qué.-Liberal

Man.-Conservative
B.C.-No federal affiliation
P.E.I.-Liberal

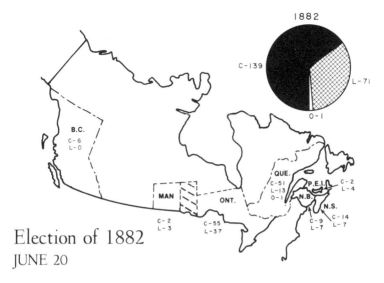

# Election of 1882
JUNE 20

**PRIME MINISTERS (PAST, PRESENT, AND FUTURE)**

Macdonald-Carleton, Ont. (E) Lennox, Ont. (E)*
Mackenzie-York East, Ont. (E)
Abbott-Argenteuil, Qué. (E)
Bowell-Hastings North, Ont. (E)
Tupper-Cumberland, N.S. (E)
Laurier-Québec East, Qué. (E)
*Resigned seat.
(E)-Elected.

**PARTY LEADERS**

Sir John A. Macdonald-Conservative
Edward Blake-Liberal

**PROVINCIAL GOVERNMENTS AT TIME OF ELECTION**

N.B.-Conservative             Man.-Conservative
N.S.-Conservative             B.C.-No federal affiliation
Ont.-Liberal                  P.E.I.-Conservative
Qué.-Conservative

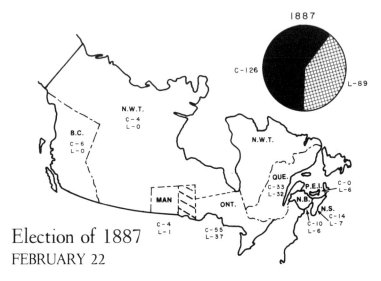

# Election of 1887
FEBRUARY 22

## PRIME MINISTERS (PAST, PRESENT, AND FUTURE)

Macdonald-Kingston, Ont. (E) Carleton, Ont. (E)*
Mackenzie-York East, Ont. (E)
Thompson-Antigonish, N.S. (E)
Bowell-Hastings North, Ont. (E)
Tupper-Cumberland, N.S. (E)
Laurier-Québec East, Qué. (E)
*Resigned seat. (E)-Elected.

## PARTY LEADERS

Sir John A. Macdonald-Conservative
Edward Blake-Liberal

## PROVINCIAL GOVERNMENTS AT TIME OF ELECTION

N.B.-Liberal                    Man.-Conservative
N.S.-Liberal                    B.C.-No federal affiliation
Ont.-Liberal                    P.E.I.-Conservative
Qué.-Liberal

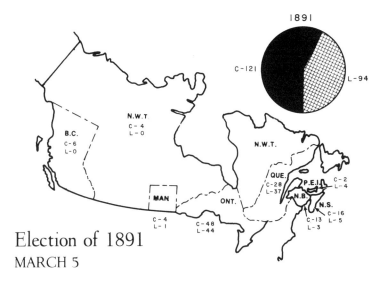

# Election of 1891
MARCH 5

**PRIME MINISTERS (PAST, PRESENT, AND FUTURE)**

Macdonald-Kingston, Ont. (E)
Mackenzie-York East, Ont. (E)
Thompson-Antigonish, N.S. (E)
Bowell-Hastings North, Ont. (E)
Laurier-Québec East, Qué. (E)
(E)-Elected.

**PARTY LEADERS**

Sir John A. Macdonald-Conservative
Sir Wilfrid Laurier-Liberal

**PROVINCIAL GOVERNMENTS AT TIME OF ELECTION**

N.B.-Liberal
N.S.-Liberal
Ont.-Liberal
Qué.-Liberal

Man.-Liberal
B.C.-No federal affiliation
P.E.I.-Conservative

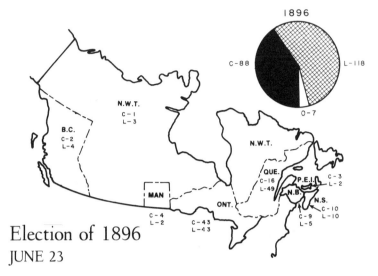

# Election of 1896
## JUNE 23

### PRIME MINISTERS (PAST, PRESENT, AND FUTURE)

Tupper-Cape Breton, N.S. (E)
Laurier-Québec East, Qué. (E) Saskatchewan, N.W.T. (E)*
Borden-Halifax, N.S. (E)

*Resigned seat.
(E)-Elected.

### PARTY LEADERS

Sir Wilfrid Laurier-Liberal
Sir Charles Tupper-Conservative

### PROVINCIAL GOVERNMENTS AT TIME OF ELECTION

| | |
|---|---|
| N.B.-Liberal | Man.-Liberal |
| N.S.-Liberal | B.C.-Liberal |
| Ont.-Liberal | P.E.I.-Liberal |
| Qué.-Conservative | |

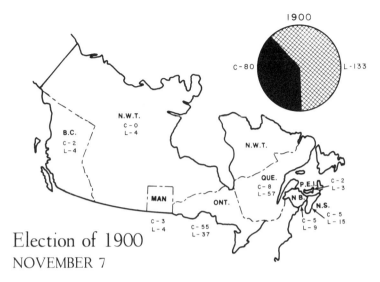

# Election of 1900
NOVEMBER 7

**PRIME MINISTERS (PAST, PRESENT, AND FUTURE)**

Tupper-Cape Breton, N.S. (D)
Laurier-Québec East, Qué. (E)
Borden-Halifax, N.S. (E)
(E)-Elected; (D)-Defeated.

**PARTY LEADERS**

Sir Wilfrid Laurier-Liberal
Sir Charles Tupper-Conservative

**PROVINCIAL GOVERNMENTS AT TIME OF ELECTION**

N.B.-Liberal            Man.-Conservative
N.S.-Liberal            B.C.-Conservative
Ont.-Liberal            P.E.I.-Liberal
Qué.-Liberal

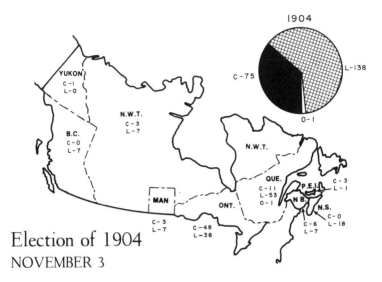

# Election of 1904
## NOVEMBER 3

### PRIME MINISTERS (PAST, PRESENT, AND FUTURE)

Laurier-Québec East, Qué. (E) Wright, Ont. (E)*
Borden-Halifax, N.S. (D)†

*Resigned seat. †Re-elected in by-election, Feb. 4, 1905 (Carleton, Ont.)
(E)-Elected, (D)-Defeated.

### PARTY LEADERS

Sir Wilfrid Laurier-Liberal
Sir Robert Borden-Conservative

### PROVINCIAL GOVERNMENTS AT TIME OF ELECTION

| | |
|---|---|
| N.B.-Liberal | Man.-Conservative |
| N.S.-Liberal | B.C.-Conservative |
| Ont.-Liberal | P.E.I.-Liberal |
| Qué.-Liberal | |

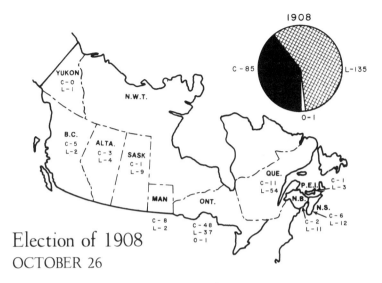

# Election of 1908
OCTOBER 26

## PRIME MINISTERS (PAST, PRESENT, AND FUTURE)

Laurier-Québec East, Qué. (E) Ottawa City, Ont. (E)*
Borden-Halifax, N.S. (E) Carleton, Ont. (E)*
Meighen-Portage la Prairie, Man. (E)
King-Waterloo North, Ont. (E)
*Resigned seat. (E)-Elected.

## PARTY LEADERS

Sir Wilfrid Laurier-Liberal
Sir Robert Borden-Conservative

## PROVINCIAL GOVERNMENTS AT TIME OF ELECTION

N.B.-Conservative              B.C.-Conservative
N.S.-Liberal                   P.E.I.-Liberal
Ont.-Conservative              Sask.-Liberal
Qué.-Liberal                   Alta.-Liberal
Man.-Conservative

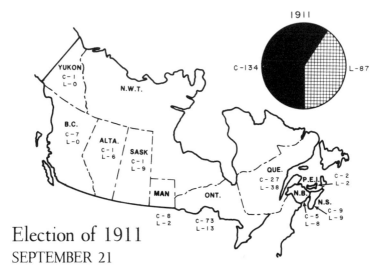

1911

C -134          L -87

YUKON
c – 1
L – 0

N.W.T.

B.C.
c – 7
L – 0

ALTA.
c – 1
L – 6

SASK
c – 1
L – 9

QUE.
c – 27
L – 38

P.E.I.
c – 2
L – 2

N.B.

N.S.
c – 9
L – 9

c – 5
L – 8

MAN

ONT.

c – 8
L – 2

c – 73
L – 13

# Election of 1911
SEPTEMBER 21

## PRIME MINISTERS (PAST, PRESENT, AND FUTURE)

Laurier-Québec East, Qué. (E)
Borden-Halifax, N.S. (E)
Meighen-Portage la Prairie, Man. (E)
King-Waterloo North, Ont. (D)
Bennett-Calgary, Alta. (E)
(E)-Elected; (D)-Defeated.

## PARTY LEADERS

Sir Robert Borden-Conservative
Sir Wilfrid Laurier-Liberal

## PROVINCIAL GOVERNMENTS AT TIME OF ELECTION

N.B.-Conservative               B.C.-Conservative
N.S.-Liberal                    P.E.I.-Liberal
Ont.-Conservative               Sask.-Liberal
Qué.-Liberal                    Alta.-Liberal
Man.-Conservative

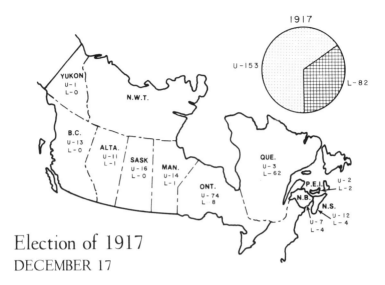

# Election of 1917
## DECEMBER 17

### PRIME MINISTERS (PAST, PRESENT, AND FUTURE)

Laurier-Québec East, Qué. (E), Ottawa City, Ont. (D)
Borden-Kings, N.S. (E)
Meighen-Portage la Prairie, Man. (E)
King-York North, Ont. (D)*
*Re-elected in by-election, Oct. 20, 1919 (P.E.I.).
(E)-Elected; (D)-Defeated.

### PARTY LEADERS
Sir Robert Borden-Unionist
Sir Wilfrid Laurier-Liberal

### PROVINCIAL GOVERNMENTS AT TIME OF ELECTION

| | |
|---|---|
| N.B.-Liberal | B.C.-Liberal |
| N.S.-Liberal | P.E.I.-Conservative |
| Ont.-Conservative | Sask.-Liberal |
| Qué.-Liberal | Alta.-Liberal |
| Man.-Liberal | |

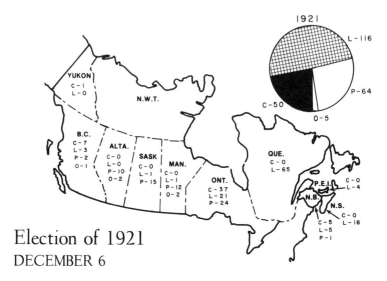

# Election of 1921
## DECEMBER 6

**PRIME MINISTERS (PAST, PRESENT, AND FUTURE)**

Meighen-Portage la Prairie, Man. (D)*
King-York North, Ont. (E)
Bennett-Calgary West, Alta. (D)
*Re-elected in by-election, Jan. 26, 1922 (Grenville, Ont.)
(E)-Elected; (D)-Defeated.

**PARTY LEADERS**

W.L. Mackenzie King-Liberal
Thomas Crerar-Progressive
Arthur Meighen-Conservative

**PROVINCIAL GOVERNMENTS AT TIME OF ELECTION**

N.B.-Liberal                    B.C.-Liberal
N.S.-Liberal                    P.E.I.-Liberal
Ont.-United Farmers             Sask.-Liberal
Qué.-Liberal                    Alta.-Liberal
Man.-Liberal

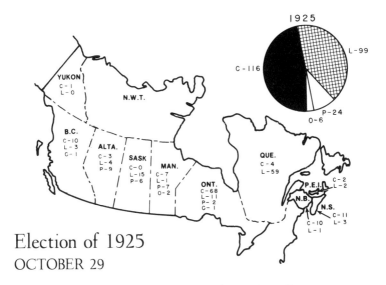

# Election of 1925
## OCTOBER 29

**PRIME MINISTERS (PAST, PRESENT, AND FUTURE)**

Meighen-Portage la Prairie, Man. (E)
King-York North, Ont. (D)*
Bennett-Calgary West, Alta. (E)
Diefenbaker-Prince Albert, Sask. (D)

*Re-elected in by-election, Feb. 15, 1926 (Prince Albert, Sask.).
(E)-Elected; (D)-Defeated.

**PARTY LEADERS**

W.L. Mackenzie King-Liberal
Arthur Meighen-Conservative
Robert Forke-Progressive

**PROVINCIAL GOVERNMENTS AT TIME OF ELECTION**

| | |
|---|---|
| N.B.-Conservative | B.C.-Liberal |
| N.S.-Liberal | P.E.I.-Conservative |
| Ont.-Conservative | Sask.-Liberal |
| Qué.-Liberal | Alta.-United Farmers |
| Man.-United Farmers | |

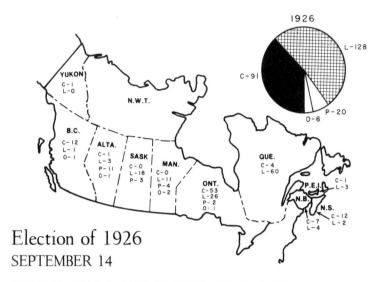

1926
L-128
C-91
O-6
P-20

YUKON
C-1
L-0

N.W.T.

B.C.
C-12
L-1
O-1

ALTA.
C-1
L-3
P-11
O-1

SASK
C-0
L-18
P-3

MAN.
C-0
L-11
P-4
O-2

ONT.
C-53
L-26
P-2
O-1

QUE.
C-4
L-60

P.E.I.
C-1
L-3

N.B.
C-7
L-4

N.S.
C-12
L-2

# Election of 1926
SEPTEMBER 14

### PRIME MINISTERS (PAST, PRESENT, AND FUTURE)

Meighen-Portage la Prairie, Man. (D)
King-Prince Albert, Sask. (E)
Bennett-Calgary West, Alta. (E)
Diefenbaker-Prince Albert, Sask. (D)
(E)-Elected; (D)-Defeated.

### PARTY LEADERS

W.L. Mackenzie King-Liberal
Arthur Meighen-Conservative
Robert Forke-Progressive

### PROVINCIAL GOVERNMENTS AT TIME OF ELECTION

N.B.-Conservative  B.C.-Liberal
N.S.-Liberal  P.E.I.-Conservative
Ont.-Conservative  Sask.-Liberal
Qué.-Liberal  Alta.-United Farmers
Man.-United Farmers

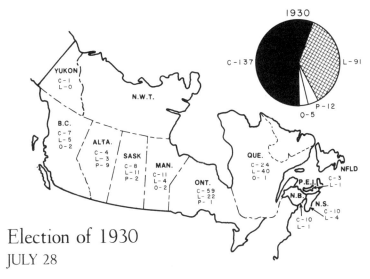

**YUKON**
C - 1
L - 0

**N.W.T.**

**B.C.**
C - 7
L - 5
O - 2

**ALTA.**
C - 4
L - 3
P - 9

**SASK**
C - 8
L - 11
P - 2

**MAN.**
C - 11
L - 4
O - 2

**ONT.**
C - 59
L - 22
P - 1

**QUE.**
C - 24
L - 40
O - 1

**NFLD**

**P.E.I.**
C - 3
L - 1

**N.B.**
C - 10
L - 1

**N.S.**
C - 10
L - 4

1930
C - 137
L - 91
P - 12
O - 5

# Election of 1930
JULY 28

**PRIME MINISTERS (PAST, PRESENT, AND FUTURE)**

King-Prince Albert, Sask. (E)
Bennett-Calgary West, Alta. (E)
(E)-Elected.

**PARTY LEADERS**

W.L. Mackenzie King-Liberal
R.B. Bennett-Conservative

**PROVINCIAL GOVERNMENTS AT TIME OF ELECTION**

N.B.-Conservative
N.S.-Liberal
Ont.-Conservative
Qué.-Liberal
Man.-United Farmers

B.C.-Conservative
P.E.I.-Liberal
Sask.-Conservative
Alta.-United Farmers

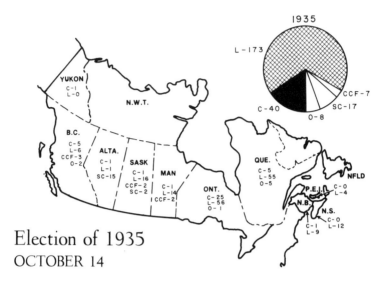

# Election of 1935
OCTOBER 14

## PRIME MINISTERS (PAST, PRESENT, AND FUTURE)

King-Prince Albert, Sask. (E)
Bennett-Calgary West, Alta. (E)
(E)-Elected.

## PARTY LEADERS

W.L. Mackenzie King-Liberal
R.B. Bennett-Conservative
J.S. Woodsworth-Co-operative Commonwealth Federation
John Blackmore-Social Credit

## PROVINCIAL GOVERNMENTS AT TIME OF ELECTION

N.B.-Liberal
N.S.-Liberal
Ont.-Liberal
Qué.-Liberal
Man.-United Farmers

B.C.-Liberal
P.E.I.-Liberal
Sask.-Liberal
Alta.-Social Credit

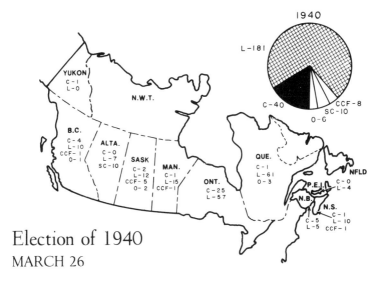

# Election of 1940
MARCH 26

**PRIME MINISTERS (PAST, PRESENT, AND FUTURE)**

King-Prince Albert, Sask. (E)
Diefenbaker-Lake Centre, Sask. (E)
(E)-Elected.

**PARTY LEADERS**

W.L. Mackenzie King-Liberal
R.J. Manion-Conservative
J.S. Woodsworth-Co-operative Commonwealth Federation
John Blackmore-Social Credit

**PROVINCIAL GOVERNMENTS AT TIME OF ELECTION**

N.B.-Liberal
N.S.-Liberal
Ont.-Liberal
Qué.-Liberal
Man.-United Farmers

B.C.-Liberal
P.E.I.-Liberal
Sask.-Liberal
Alta.-Social Credit

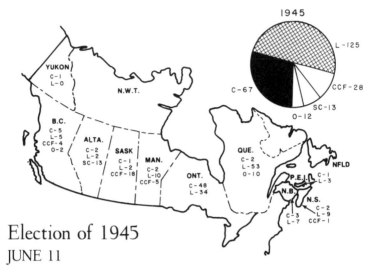

# Election of 1945
## JUNE 11

**PRIME MINISTERS (PAST, PRESENT, AND FUTURE)**

King-Prince Albert, Sask. (D)*
St. Laurent-Québec East, Qué. (E)
Diefenbaker-Lake Centre, Sask. (E)

*Re-elected in by-election, Aug. 6, 1945 (Glengarry, Ont.).
(E)-Elected; (D)-Defeated.

**PARTY LEADERS**

W.L. Mackenzie King-Liberal
John Bracken-Conservative
M.J. Coldwell-Co-operative Commonwealth Federation
Solon Low-Social Credit

**PROVINCIAL GOVERNMENTS AT TIME OF ELECTION**

| | |
|---|---|
| N.B.-Liberal | B.C.-Coalition |
| N.S.-Liberal | P.E.I.-Liberal |
| Ont.-Conservative | Sask.-Co-operative |
| Qué.-Union Nationale |     Commonwealth Federation |
| Man.-Coalition | Alta.-Social Credit |

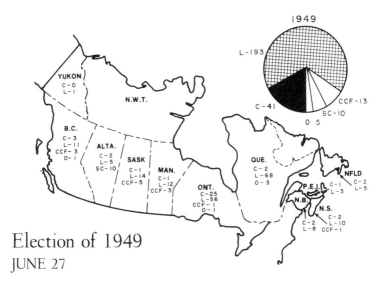

# Election of 1949

JUNE 27

## PRIME MINISTERS (PAST, PRESENT, AND FUTURE)

St. Laurent-Québec East, Qué. (E)
Diefenbaker-Lake Centre, Sask. (E)
Pearson-Algoma East, Ont. (E)
(E)-Elected.

## PARTY LEADERS

Louis St. Laurent-Liberal
George Drew-Conservative
M.J. Coldwell-Co-operative Commonwealth Federation
Solon Low-Social Credit

## PROVINCIAL GOVERNMENTS AT TIME OF ELECTION

N.B.-Liberal
N.S.-Liberal
Ont.-Conservative
Man.-Coalition
B.C.-Coalition

P.E.I.-Liberal
Sask.-Co-operative
  Commonwealth Federation
Alta.-Social Credit

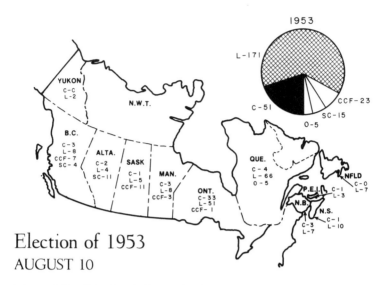

# Election of 1953
## AUGUST 10

**PRIME MINISTERS (PAST, PRESENT, AND FUTURE)**

St. Laurent-Québec East, Qué. (E)
Diefenbaker-Prince Albert, Sask. (E)
Pearson-Algoma East, Ont. (E)
(E)-Elected.

**PARTY LEADERS**

Louis St. Laurent-Liberal
George Drew-Conservative
M.J. Coldwell-Co-operative Commonwealth Federation
Solon Low-Social Credit

**PROVINCIAL GOVERNMENTS AT TIME OF ELECTION**

N.B.-Conservative
N.S.-Liberal
Ont.-Conservative
Qué.-Union Nationale
Man.-Coalition
B.C.-Social Credit

P.E.I.-Liberal
Sask.-Co-operative
Commonwealth Federation
Alta.-Social Credit
Nfld.-Liberal

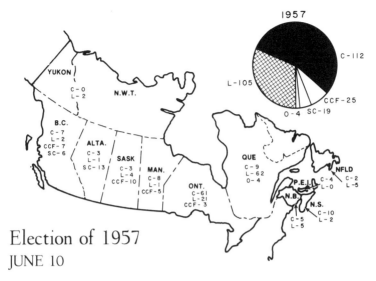

1957

C-112
L-105
CCF-25
0-4  SC-19

YUKON
C-0
L-2

N.W.T.

B.C.
C-7
L-2
CCF-7
SC-6

ALTA.
C-3
L-1
SC-13

SASK
C-3
L-4
CCF-10

MAN.
C-8
L-1
CCF-5

ONT.
C-61
L-21
CCF-3

QUE
C-9
L-62
0-4

NFLD
C-2
L-5

P.E.I.
C-4
L-0

N.B.
C-5
L-5

N.S.
C-10
L-2

# Election of 1957
JUNE 10

**PRIME MINISTERS (PAST, PRESENT, AND FUTURE)**

St. Laurent-Québec East, Qué. (E)
Diefenbaker-Prince Albert, Sask. (E)
Pearson-Algoma East, Ont. (E)
(E)-Elected.

**PARTY LEADERS**

John Diefenbaker-Conservative
Louis St. Laurent-Liberal
M.J. Coldwell-Co-operative Commonwealth Federation
Solon Low-Social Credit

**PROVINCIAL GOVERNMENTS AT TIME OF ELECTION**

N.B.-Conservative
N.S.-Conservative
Ont.-Conservative
Qué.-Union Nationale
Man.-Coalition
B.C.-Social Credit

P.E.I.-Liberal
Sask.-Co-operative
Commonwealth Federation
Alta.-Social Credit
Nfld.-Liberal

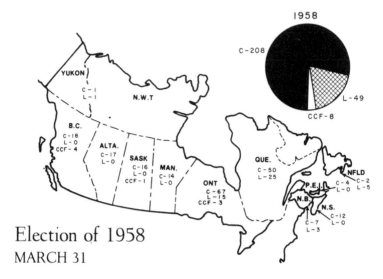

# Election of 1958
MARCH 31

**PRIME MINISTERS (PAST, PRESENT, AND FUTURE)**

Diefenbaker-Prince Albert, Sask. (E)
Pearson-Algoma East, Ont. (E)
(E)-Elected.

**PARTY LEADERS**

John Diefenbaker-Conservative
Lester Pearson-Liberal
M.J. Coldwell-Co-operative Commonwealth Federation

**PROVINCIAL GOVERNMENTS AT TIME OF ELECTION**

N.B.-Conservative                    P.E.I.-Liberal
N.S.-Conservative                    Sask.-Co-operative
Ont.-Conservative                    Commonwealth Federation
Qué.-Union Nationale                 Alta.-Social Credit
Man.-Coalition                       Nfld.-Liberal
B.C.-Social Credit

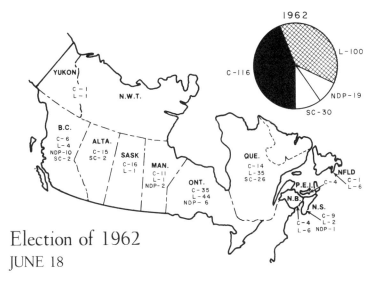

# Election of 1962
JUNE 18

**PRIME MINISTERS (PAST, PRESENT, AND FUTURE)**

Diefenbaker-Prince Albert, Sask. (E)
Pearson-Algoma East (E)
(E)-Elected.

**PARTY LEADERS**

John Diefenbaker-Conservative
Lester Pearson-Liberal
T.C. Douglas-New Democratic Party (formerly CCF)
Robert Thompson-Social Credit

**PROVINCIAL GOVERNMENTS AT TIME OF ELECTION**

| | |
|---|---|
| N.B.-Liberal | P.E.I.-Conservative |
| N.S.-Conservative | Sask.-Co-operative |
| Ont.-Conservative | Commonwealth Federation-New |
| Qué.-Liberal | Democratic Party |
| Man.-Conservative | Alta.-Social Credit |
| B.C.-Social Credit | Nfld.-Liberal |

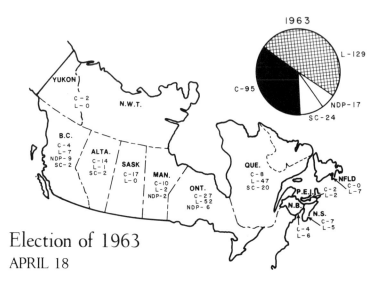

# Election of 1963
APRIL 18

## PRIME MINISTERS (PAST, PRESENT, AND FUTURE)

Diefenbaker-Prince Albert, Sask. (E)
Pearson-Algoma East, Ont. (E)
(E)-Elected.

## PARTY LEADERS

Lester Pearson-Liberal
John Diefenbaker-Conservative
T.C. Douglas-New Democratic Party
Robert Thompson-Social Credit

## PROVINCIAL GOVERNMENTS AT TIME OF ELECTION

N.B.-Liberal
N.S.-Conservative
Ont.-Conservative
Qué.-Liberal
Man.-Conservative
B.C.-Social Credit

P.E.I.-Conservative
Sask.-Co-operative
Commonwealth Federation-New
Democratic Party
Alta.-Social Credit
Nfld.-Liberal

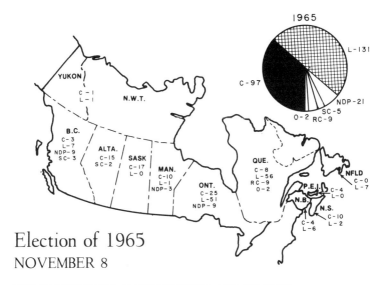

# Election of 1965

NOVEMBER 8

### PRIME MINISTERS (PAST, PRESENT, AND FUTURE)

Diefenbaker-Prince Albert, Sask. (E)
Pearson-Algoma East, Ont. (E)
Trudeau-Mount Royal, Qué. (E)
(E)-Elected.

### PARTY LEADERS

Lester Pearson-Liberal
John Diefenbaker-Conservative
T.C. Douglas-New Democratic Party
Robert Thompson-Social Credit
Réal Caouette-Créditistes

### PROVINCIAL GOVERNMENTS AT TIME OF ELECTION

| | |
|---|---|
| N.B.-Liberal | B.C.-Social Credit |
| N.S.-Conservative | P.E.I.-Conservative |
| Ont.-Conservative | Sask.-Liberal |
| Qué.-Liberal | Alta.-Social Credit |
| Man.-Conservative | Nfld.-Liberal |

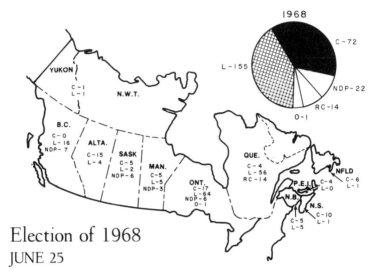

# Election of 1968
JUNE 25

**PRIME MINISTERS (PAST, PRESENT, AND FUTURE)**

Diefenbaker-Prince Albert, Sask. (E)
Trudeau-Mount Royal, Qué. (E)
(E)-Elected.

**PARTY LEADERS**

Pierre E. Trudeau-Liberal
Robert Stanfield-Conservative
T.C. Douglas-New Democratic Party
A.B. Patterson-Social Credit
Réal Caouette-Créditistes

**PROVINCIAL GOVERNMENTS AT TIME OF ELECTION**

| | |
|---|---|
| N.B.-Liberal | B.C.-Social Credit |
| N.S.-Conservative | P.E.I.-Liberal |
| Ont.-Conservative | Sask.-Liberal |
| Qué.-Union Nationale | Alta.-Social Credit |
| Man.-Conservative | Nfld.-Liberal |

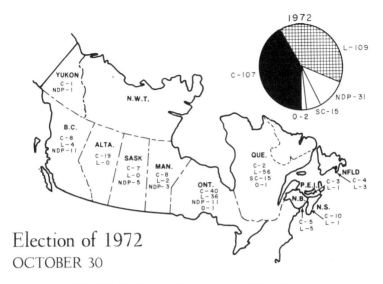

# Election of 1972
OCTOBER 30

## PRIME MINISTERS (PAST, PRESENT, AND FUTURE)

Diefenbaker-Prince Albert, Sask. (E)
Trudeau-Mount Royal, Qué. (E)
Clark-Yellowhead, Alta. (E)
(E)-Elected.

## PARTY LEADERS

Pierre E. Trudeau-Liberal
Robert Stanfield-Conservative
David Lewis-New Democratic Party
Réal Caouette-Social Credit

## PROVINCIAL GOVERNMENTS AT TIME OF ELECTION

N.B.-Conservative
N.S.-Liberal
Ont.-Conservative
Qué.-Liberal
Man.-New Democratic Party

B.C.-New Democratic Party
P.E.I.-Liberal
Sask.-New Democratic Party
Alta.-Conservative
Nfld.-Conservative

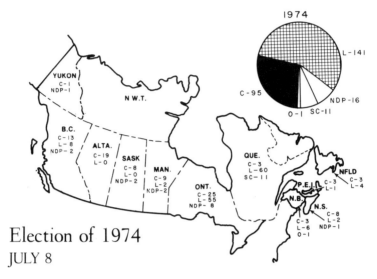

# Election of 1974
## JULY 8

**PRIME MINISTERS (PAST, PRESENT, AND FUTURE)**

Diefenbaker-Prince Albert, Sask. (E)
Trudeau-Mount Royal, Qué. (E)
Clark-Yellowhead, Alta. (E)
(E)-Elected.

**PARTY LEADERS**

Pierre E. Trudeau-Liberal
Robert Stanfield-Conservative
David Lewis-New Democratic Party
Réal Caouette-Social Credit

**PROVINCIAL GOVERNMENTS AT TIME OF ELECTION**

| | |
|---|---|
| N.B.-Conservative | B.C.-New Democratic Party |
| N.S.-Liberal | P.E.I.-Liberal |
| Ont.-Conservative | Sask.-New Democratic Party |
| Qué.-Liberal | Alta.-Conservative |
| Man.-New Democratic Party | Nfld.-Liberal |

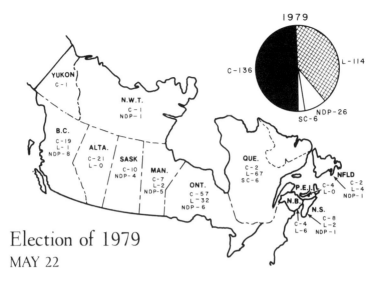

# Election of 1979
## MAY 22

### PRIME MINISTERS (PAST, PRESENT, AND FUTURE)

Diefenbaker-Prince Albert, Sask. (E)
Trudeau-Mount Royal, Qué. (E)
Clark-Yellowhead, Alta. (E)
(E)-Elected.

### PARTY LEADERS

Joseph Clark-Conservative
Pierre E. Trudeau-Liberal
Edward Broadbent-New Democratic Party
Fabien Roy-Social Credit

### PROVINCIAL GOVERNMENTS AT TIME OF ELECTION

N.B.-Conservative      B.C.-Social Credit
N.S.-Conservative      P.E.I.-Conservative
Ont.-Conservative      Sask.-New Democratic Party
Qué.-Parti Québécois      Alta.-Conservative
Man.-Conservative      Nfld.-Liberal

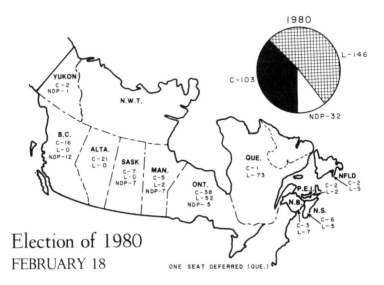

# Election of 1980
## FEBRUARY 18

ONE SEAT DEFERRED (QUE.)

### PRIME MINISTERS (PAST, PRESENT, AND FUTURE)

Trudeau-Mount Royal, Qué. (E)
Clark-Yellowhead, Alta. (E)
(E)-Elected

### PARTY LEADERS

Pierre E. Trudeau-Liberal
Joseph Clark-Conservative
Edward Broadbent-New Democratic Party
Fabien Roy-Social Credit

### PROVINCIAL GOVERNMENTS AT TIME OF ELECTION

| | |
|---|---|
| N.B.-Conservative | B.C.-Social Credit |
| N.S.-Conservative | P.E.I.-Conservative |
| Ont.-Conservative | Sask.-New Democratic Party |
| Qué.-Parti Québécois | Alta.-Conservative |
| Man.-Conservative | Nfld.-Liberal |

# THREE

# Twentieth-Century
# Party Leaders and Current Premiers

Not everyone can be prime minister, and this section deals primarily with many who aspired to the job but failed. It may not always be true that the best man won.

This section also takes note of the current provincial premiers. Whether their future will carry them to higher office, only time will tell.

# Twentieth-Century Party Leaders and Current Premiers

**Aberhart, William** (1878-1943) Premier of Alberta (1935-1943), founder and leader of Social Credit party (1932-1943).

**Argue, Hazen** (b. 1921) Member of Parliament (1945-1963), CCF president and leader (1960-1962), member of Senate (1966-present).

**Bennett, William R.** (b. 1932) Businessman, member of British Columbia Legislature (1973-present), leader of Social Credit party (1973-present), premier (1975-present).

**Blakeney, Allan** (b. 1925) Lawyer, member of Saskatchewan Legislature (1960-present), leader of New Democratic party (1970-present), premier (1971-1982), defeated as premier April 26, 1982.

**Bracken, John** (1883-1969) Premier of Manitoba (1922-1943), member of Parliament (1945-1949), leader of Conservative party (1942-1948), leader of opposition (1945-1948).

**Broadbent, Edward** (b. 1936) Member of House of Commons (1968-present), leader of New Democratic party (1975-present).

**Buchanan, John** (b. 1931) Lawyer, member of Nova Scotia Legislature (1967-present), leader of Conservative party

(1971-present), premier (1978-present).

**Buck, Tim** (1891-1973) Leader of Communist party of Canada (1929-1962).

**Caouette, Réal** (1917-1976) Member of Parliament (1946-1949, 1962-1976), leader of Créditistes party (1963-1971), leader of Social Credit party (1971-1976).

**Coldwell, Major James William** (1888-1974) Member of Parliament (1935-1958), parliamentary leader of CCF party (1940-1958), national president of CCF party (1942-1960).

**Crerar, T.A.** (1876-1975) Member of Parliament (1917-1922, 1930, 1935-1945), leader of Progressive party (1920-1922), member of the Senate (1945-1966).

**Davis, William** (b. 1929) Lawyer, member of Ontario Legislature (1959-present), leader of Conservative party (1971-present), premier (1971-present).

**Devine, Grant** (b. 1945) Professor, leader of Saskatchewan Conservative party (1972-present), premier (1982-present).

**Douglas, Thomas** (b. 1904) Premier of Saskatchewan (1944-1961), member of Parliament (1935-1944, 1962-1968, 1969-1979), leader of New Democratic party (1961-1971).

**Drew, George** (1894-1973) Premier of Ontario (1943-1948), member of Parliament (1948-1957), leader of Conservative party and leader of the opposition (1948-1956).

**Forke, Robert** (1860-1934) Member of Parliament (1921-1929), House leader of Progressive party (1922-1926), member of Senate (1929-1934).

**Fortin, André** (b. 1943) Member of Parliament (1965-1979), leader of Social Credit party (1976-1979).

**Guthrie, Hugh** (1866-1939) Member of Parliament (1900-1935), temporary leader of Conservative party (1926-1927).

**Hanson, Richard** (1879-1948) Member of Parliament (1921-1935, 1940-1945), leader of Conservative party in House of Commons (1940-43).

**Hatfield, Richard B.** (b. 1931) Lawyer/businessman, member of New Brunswick Legislature (1961-present), leader of Conservative party (1969-present), premier (1970-present).

**Lee, James** (b. 1937) Realtor, member of Prince Edward Island Legislature (1975-present), premier (1981-present).

**Lévesque, René** (b. 1922) Journalist, member of Québec Legislature (1960-1970, 1976-present), leader of Parti Québécois (1968-present), premier (1976-present).

**Lewis, David** (1909-1981) Member of Parliament (1965-1974), leader of New Democratic party (1971-1975).

**Lougheed, Peter** (b. 1928) Lawyer, member of Alberta Legislature (1967-present), leader of Conservative party (1966-present), premier (1971-present).

**Low, Solon** (1900-1962) Member of Parliament (1945-1958), leader of Social Credit party (1948-1958).

**Lyon, Sterling R.** (b. 1927) Lawyer, member of Manitoba Legislature (1958-1969, 1976-present), leader of Conservative party (1975-present), premier (1977-1981), defeated as premier Nov. 17, 1981.

**MacLean, J. Angus** (b. 1914) Farmer, member of House of Commons (1951-1976), member of Prince Edward Island Legislature (1977-present), premier (1979-1981), resigned as premier Nov. 7, 1981.

**Manion, Robert** (1881-1943) Member of Parliament (1917-1935), leader of Conservative party (1938-1940).

**Mulroney, Brian** (b. 1939) Lawyer, member of Parliament (1983-present), leader of Conservative party and leader of the opposition (1983-present).

**Pawley, Howard** (b. 1943) Lawyer, member of Manitoba Legislature (1969-present), New Democratic party leader (1979-present), premier (1982-present).

**Peckford, A. Brian** (b. 1942) Teacher, member of Newfoundland Legislature (1972-present), leader of Conservative party (1979-present), premier (1979-present).

**Roy, Fabien** (b. 1928) Member of Parliament (1974-1980), leader of Social Credit party (1979-1980).

**Stanfield, Robert** (b. 1914) Premier of Nova Scotia (1956-1967), leader of Conservative party and leader of the opposition (1967-1976).

**Thompson, Robert** (b. 1914) Member of Parliament (1962-1968 as Social Credit; 1968-1972 as Conservative), leader of Social Credit party (1961-1967).

# FOUR

# Quotable Quotes

Public office offers one the opportunity to be oft-quoted. This section deals with prime ministerial quotes best remembered or, perhaps, forgotten.

A spirit of nationalism, a prophetic statement, an ill-advised comment, or a touch of humour usually places one's words on the lips of others.

# Quotable Quotes

## Sir John A. Macdonald

"Let us be English or let us be French, but above all let us be Canadians."

"A British subject I was born. A British subject I will die."

"Give me better wood, and I will make you a better cabinet."

[No government positions for] "overwashed Englishmen utterly ignorant of the country and full of crotches as all Englishmen are."

"Anybody can support me when I am right. What I want is a man to support me when I am wrong."

"A compliment is a statement of an agreeable truth; flattery is the statement of an agreeable untruth."

"Any election is like a horserace in that you can tell more about it the next day."

"The time has come, I think, when we must choose men for their qualifications rather than their localities."

"Oh, take me home." (*last words*)

## Alexander Mackenzie

"To elevate that standard of public morality." (*after Pacific scandal*)

"Loyalty to the queen does not require a man to bow down to her manservant, or her maidservant, or her ass."

"I am ambitious to succeed in governing the county well and

without any reproach, but beyond that my ambition is of a very humble kind."

"To legislate in advance of public opinion is merely to produce anarchy instead of maintaining law and order."

## Sir John Abbott

"Because I am not particularly obnoxious to anybody." (*Abbott commenting on why he was chosen as prime minister.*)

"I hate politics."

## Sir John Thompson

"He who serves Canada serves the Empire, and he who serves the Empire serves Canada as well."

"These Yankee politicians are the lowest race of thieves in existence."

"Oh pray do not bother to close the window. I think they are all in now." (*on mosquitoes*)

## Sir Mackenzie Bowell

"A nest of traitors." (*Referring to seven resigning Cabinet members*)

## Sir Charles Tupper

"What Canada wants is a national policy."

"It requires a great country and great circumstances to develop great men."

"The Pacific Slander." (*referring to the Pacific scandal*)

## Sir Wilfrid Laurier

"I am English to the core."

"Either England must advance, or Canada recede."

"Canada first, Canada last, Canada always."

"The twentieth century belongs to Canada."

"The Liberal party is broad enough, Liberal principals large enough to give an equal share of justice and liberty to all men."

"I am branded in Québec as a traitor to the French and in Ontario as a traitor to the English."

"For us, sons of France, political sentiment is a passion, while for the Englishman, politics are a question of business."

"The great mass of the electors are ignorant."

"So long as there are French mothers, that language will not die."

"Québec does not have opinions, but only sentiments."


## Sir Robert Borden

"The British Empire first, and, within the British Empire, Canada first."

"I conceive that women are entitled to the franchise on their merits."

"Canada does not propose to be an adjunct even of the British Empire, but, as has been well and eloquently expressed, to be a greater part in a greater whole."

"As the pen is mightier than the sword, so are brains mightier than the muscles."

## Arthur Meighen

"Difficulties do not crush men, they make them."

"Ready aye ready; we stand by you." (*showing support for England*)

"Facts never collide; in their long procession there is always harmony from the first movement to the last."

"The story of a nation's heroes is the fountain from which it draws the wine of its later life."

## W.L. Mackenzie King

"Not necessarily conscription, but conscription if necessary."

"I would not give one cent to any Tory government." (*to Conservative-controlled provincial legislatures*)

"Poverty and adversity, want and misery are the enemies which liberalism will seek to banish from our land."

"In matters between Canada and other countries, Canada should arrange her own affairs."

"We are fortunate both in our neighbours and in our lack of neighbours."

"If some countries have too much history, we have too much geography."

"The promises of yesterday are the taxes of today."

## R.B. Bennett

"The West is not thinking, the West is drinking."

"One of the greatest assets any man or woman can have on

entering life's struggle is poverty."

"I am for the British Empire after Canada."

"Amalgamation never! Competition ever!" (*on* C.N.R.)

## Louis St. Laurent

"They have just got tired of seeing us around." (*after* 1957 *election defeat*)

"For people like him Canada has never been and will never be anything but a conquered colony." (*speaking of former Prime Minister Arthur Meighen*)

"The first duty of a Canadian is not toward the British Commonwealth but toward Canada and its king."

"Socialists are Liberals in a hurry."

## John Diefenbaker

"My fellow Canadians . . ."

"A Canadian I was born and a Canadian I will die."

"The duty of the opposition is to turn out the government."

"To the young members who have just come, I would say that, for the next six months after you are here, you will wonder how you got here. Then after that you will wonder how the rest of the members got here."

"I have sometimes been wrong; I have never been on the side of wrong."

"I've lived history. I've made history, and I know I'll have my place in history."

"I never campaign. I just visit with the people."

"I see a new Canada, a Canada of the North."

"We shall be Canadians first, foremost, and always."

## Lester Pearson

"This is the flag of the future, but it does not dishonour the past."

"Not to seek success, but to deserve it."

"I didn't say what I said when I said it. What I meant to say when I didn't say it was that I wouldn't have said what I said when I did say it."

"A Liberal is a man of the centre moving forward."

## Pierre Trudeau

"Fuddle-duddle" (*obscene and not heard*)

"Separatism is against the gut interest and the gut feeling of the average Canadian."

"The state has no place in the nation's bedroom."

"We will gain little respect from others, least of all from the Americans, if we do not have the courage and the self-confidence to act as Canadians."

"I believe in the unity of Canada. I believe that Canada is one country, and that Canadians are one people."

"When you howl like animals, I cannot hear very well the questions you are asking." (*to opposition members in Commons*)

"Living next to you is in some ways like sleeping with an elephant." (*on the relationship between Canada and the United States*)

## Joseph Clark

"I am full of confidence about this party and this country. Let us get on with the job of building Canada."

"If I'm beaten, it will be because of image." (1980)

"This is the party of the future, this is the party of victory."

"I've come to the view that the party's interest and mine are best served by my staying on in the active leadership of the party and leading us to victory."

"If we don't live up to our promises, we're dead."

"We must face the fact that differences of language and culture tend to divide, not to unite."

"The way to build a whole nation is to respect our individual parts."

## One on One

"A steam engine in striped pants." (*T. Douglas on Bennett*)

"One man government." (*King on Bennett*)

"Mackenzie King is doing excellent work, and I believe that he has quite a political future before him." (*Laurier on King, 1909*)

"Nice chap that if I were twenty years younger, he'd be my colleague." (*Macdonald on Laurier*)

"Sir John Macdonald now belongs to the ages." (*Laurier on Macdonald*)

"We loved him for the enemies he had made." (*Laurier on Mackenzie*)

"Thompson has two faults. He is a little too fond of satire and a little too much of a Nova Scotian." (*Macdonald on Thompson*)

"Sir Wilfrid is too English for me." (*Tupper on Laurier*)

"The most contemptible charlatan ever to darken the annals of Canadian politics." (*Meighen on King*)

"Pope Pearson." (*Trudeau on Pearson*)

"Hello, Mr. Wilson." (*President Johnson to Prime Minister Pearson*)

"I respect his abilities, his toughness, and his pragmatism." (*Pearson on Trudeau*)

"The more I see of St. Laurent, the nobler I believe him to be. One of God's gentlemen if ever there was one." (*King on St. Laurent*)

New member on completion of maiden speech: "People had asked why I did not speak."
R.B. Bennett: "That is better than having them ask, 'Why did you speak?'"

"I honour him as a man." (*King on Bennett*)

"I am getting past the time when I can fight in public with a man of Meighen's type who is sarcastic, vitriolic, and the meanest type of politican." (*King on Meighen*)

"The public prefers John A. drunk to his enemies sober." (*Macdonald on Macdonald*)

"The chief characteristic of Tupper was courage." (*Laurier on Tupper*)

"Behind every successful man, there is a surprised woman." (*Mrs. Pearson*)

"The only minister sticking with Trudeau is Billy Graham." (*Stanfield on Trudeau*)

"There, but for the grace of Pierre Elliott Trudeau, goes God."
(*David Lewis on Trudeau*)

"In this game you have to be a bit of an S.O.B. Joe doesn't quite
have it." (*Jim Coutts on Joe Clark*)

"If there were no other rewards in public life than to have done
what was stated by the brilliant Joe Clark." (*Diefenbaker on
Clark*)

"Canada celebrated the Year of the Child by electing Joe
Clark." (*Diefenbaker on Clark*)

"I don't consider Trudeau a representative Canadian; He is
much to rational to be French, too inflexible to be Anglo-
Saxon." (*Clark on Trudeau*)


# Election Slogans, Official and Popular

1867 "Union and Progress" (Conservative)

1878 "National Policy" (Conservative)
"Party of Purity" (Liberal)

1891 "The Old Man, the Old Flag, and the Old Policy"
(Conservative)

1896 "Land for the Settler and Not for the Speculator"
(Liberal)

1904 "Canada First, Always Canada" (Liberal)
"Land for the People" (Conservative)

1908 "Let Laurier Finish His Work" (Liberal)
"Let Laurier's Work Finish Him" (Conservative)

1911 "No Truck nor Trade with the Yankees" (Conservative)

"A Vote for Borden is a Vote for King, Flag, and Country" (Conservative)

"Laurier Prosperity" (Liberal)

1917 "A Vote for Laurier Is a Vote for the Kaiser" (Conservative)

1921 "Hark the Herald Angels Sing, William Lyon Mackenzie King" (Liberal)
"Meighen Will Lead Us Through" (Conservative)

1926 "Put King Back, and Keep Prosperity" (Liberal)
"Canada for the Canadians" (Conservative)

1930 "Canada First, Then the Empire" (Conservative)
"Let Uncle Sam go his own way. Our way is with John Bull." (Liberal)

1935 "It's King, or Chaos" (Liberal)

1940 "Let Fighting Bob [Manion] Take Hold" (Conservative)

1945 "Vote Liberal and Keep Building a New Social Order in Canada" (Liberal)

1957 "You Never Had It So Good" (Liberal)
"It's Time for a Change" (Conservative)

1958 "Vote the Pearson Plan . . . for Jobs . . . for Peace" (Liberal)

1963 "Sixty Days of Decision" (Liberal)
"I Like Mike" (Liberal)
"Man of Decision" (Pearson, Liberal)

1965 "One Canada" (Conservative)

1968 "The Just Society" (Liberal)

1979 "Joe Who" (Liberal)

# FIVE

# The Provinces

Many men have chosen to remain on the provincial scene and they should not be ignored. Many have achieved greatness and will be remembered, while others have quickly faded from view.

Early provincial party lines were not as defined as they are today. For the sake of clarity, for the post-Confederation period, federal party labels have been used when provincial parties supported federal governments in policy, if not in name.

# Provincial Governments

## Alberta Administrations

| | |
|---|---|
| Alex. Rutherford (L) | 1905-1910 |
| A.L. Sifton (L) | 1910-1917 |
| Charles Stewart (L) | 1917-1921 |
| Herbert Greenfield (UFA) | 1921-1925 |
| John Edward Brownlee (UFA) | 1925-1934 |
| Richard Gavin Reid (UFA) | 1934-1935 |
| William Aberhart (SC) | 1935-1943 |
| Ernest C. Manning (SC) | 1943-1968 |
| Harry E. Strom (SC) | 1968-1971 |
| E. Peter Lougheed (C) | 1971-present |

## British Columbia Administrations

| | |
|---|---|
| J.F. McCreight (C) | 1871-1872 |
| A. DeCosmos (C) | 1872-1874 |
| G.A. Walkem (C) | 1874-1876 |
| A.C. Elliott (C) | 1876-1878 |
| G.A. Walkem (C) | 1878-1882 |
| R. Beaven (C) | 1882-1883 |
| W. Smithe (C) | 1883-1887 |
| A.E.B. Davie (C) | 1887-1889 |
| J. Robson (L) | 1889-1892 |
| T. Davie (C) | 1892-1895 |
| J.H. Turner (C) | 1895-1898 |
| C.A. Semlin (C) | 1898-1900 |
| Joseph Martin (C) | 1900 |

| | |
|---|---|
| J. Dunsmuir (L) | 1900-1902 |
| E.G. Prior (C) | 1902-1903 |
| R. McBride (C) | 1903-1915 |
| Wm. J. Bowser (C) | 1915-1916 |
| Harlan C. Brewster (L) | 1916-1918 |
| John Olivier (L) | 1918-1927 |
| John Duncan MacLean (L) | 1927-1928 |
| Simon Fraser Tolmie (C) | 1928-1933 |
| T.D. Pattullo (L) | 1933-1941 |
| John Hart (Coalition) | 1941-1947 |
| Johnson-Anscomb (Coalition) | 1947-1952 |
| Theo. Johnson (Coalition) | 1952 |
| William Andrew Cecil Bennett (SC) | 1952-1972 |
| David Barrett (NDP) | 1972-1975 |
| William Richards Bennett (SC) | 1975-present |

## Manitoba Administrations

| | |
|---|---|
| A. Boyd (C) | 1870-1871 |
| M.A. Girard (C) | 1871-1872 |
| H.J.H. Clarke (C) | 1872-1874 |
| M.A. Girard (C) | 1874 |
| R.A. Davis (C) | 1874-1878 |
| John Norquay (C) | 1878-1887 |
| D.H. Harrison (C) | 1887-1888 |
| T. Greenway (L) | 1888-1900 |
| H.J. Macdonald (C) | 1900 |
| Sir R.P. Roblin (C) | 1900-1915 |
| T.C. Norris (L) | 1915-1922 |
| John Bracken (UF) | 1922-1943 |
| S.S. Garson (Coalition) | 1943-1948 |

| | |
|---|---|
| D.L. Campbell (Coalition) | 1948-1958 |
| Dufferin Roblin (C) | 1958-1967 |
| Walter Weir (C) | 1967-1969 |
| Edward Schreyer (NDP) | 1969-1977 |
| Sterling R. Lyon (C) | 1977-1981 |
| Howard Russell Pawley (NDP) | 1981-present |

## New Brunswick Administrations

| | |
|---|---|
| A.R. Wetmore (CF) | 1867-1870 |
| G.E. King (C) | 1870-1971 |
| George Hathaway (C) | 1871-1872 |
| G.E. King (C) | 1872-1878 |
| J.J. Fraser (C) | 1878-1882 |
| D.L. Hanington (C) | 1882-1883 |
| A.G. Blair (L) | 1883-1896 |
| Jas. Mitchell (L) | 1896-1897 |
| H.R. Emmerson (L) | 1897-1900 |
| L.J. Tweedie (L) | 1900-1907 |
| William Pugsley (L) | 1907 |
| C.W. Robinson (L) | 1907-1908 |
| J.D. Hazen (C) | 1908-1911 |
| James K. Flemming (C) | 1911-1914 |
| George J. Clarke (C) | 1914-1917 |
| James A. Murray (C) | 1917 |
| Walter E. Foster (L) | 1917-1923 |
| Peter J. Veniot (L) | 1923-1925 |
| John B.M. Baxter (C) | 1925-1931 |
| Charles D. Richards (C) | 1931-1933 |
| L.P.D. Tilley (C) | 1933-1935 |
| A. Allison Dysart (L) | 1935-1940 |
| J.B. McNair (L) | 1940-1952 |

| | |
|---|---|
| H.J. Flemming (C) | 1952-1960 |
| Louis J. Robichaud (L) | 1960-1970 |
| Richard B. Hatfield (C) | 1970-present |

## Newfoundland Administrations

| | |
|---|---|
| Joseph R. Smallwood (L) | 1949-1972 |
| Frank Duff Moores (C) | 1972-1979 |
| A. Brian Peckford (C) | 1979-present |

## Nova Scotia Administrations

| | |
|---|---|
| H. Blanchard (C) | 1867 |
| William Annand (L) | 1867-1875 |
| P.C. Hill (L) | 1875-1878 |
| S.H. Holmes (C) | 1878-1882 |
| J.S.D. Thompson (C) | 1882 |
| W.T. Pipes (L) | 1882-1884 |
| W.S. Fielding (L) | 1884-1896 |
| George H. Murray (L) | 1896-1923 |
| Ernest Howard Armstong (L) | 1923-1925 |
| Edgar N. Rhodes (C) | 1925-1930 |
| Col. Gordon S. Harrington (C) | 1930-1933 |
| A.L. Macdonald (L) | 1933-1940 |
| A.S. MacMillan (L) | 1940-1945 |
| A.L. Macdonald (L) | 1945-1954 |
| Harold Connolly (L) | 1954 |
| Henry D. Hicks (L) | 1954-1956 |
| Robert L. Stanfield (C) | 1956-1967 |
| George I. Smith (C) | 1967-1970 |
| Gerald A. Regan (L) | 1970-1978 |
| John M. Buchanan (C) | 1978-present |

## Ontario Administrations

| | |
|---|---|
| J.S. Macdonald (Coalition) | 1867-1871 |
| E. Blake (L) | 1871-1872 |
| O. Mowat (L) | 1872-1896 |
| A.S. Hardy (L) | 1896-1899 |
| G.W. Ross (L) | 1899-1905 |
| Sir J.P. Whitney (C) | 1905-1914 |
| Sir William Howard Hearst (C) | 1914-1919 |
| Ernest Charles Drury (UF) | 1919-1923 |
| G.H. Ferguson (C) | 1923-1930 |
| G.S. Henry (C) | 1930-1934 |
| M.F. Hepburn (L) | 1934-1942 |
| G.D. Conant (L) | 1942-1943 |
| H.C. Nixon (L) | 1943 |
| George A. Drew (C) | 1943-1948 |
| T.L. Kennedy (C) | 1948-1949 |
| Leslie Frost (C) | 1949-1961 |
| John P. Robarts (C) | 1961-1971 |
| William G. Davis (C) | 1971-present |

## Prince Edward Island Administrations

| | |
|---|---|
| J.C. Pope (C) | 1873 |
| L.C. Owen (C) | 1873-1876 |
| L.H. Davies (L) | 1876-1879 |
| W.W. Sullivan (C) | 1879-1889 |
| N. McLeod (C) | 1889-1891 |
| F. Peters (L) | 1891-1897 |
| A.B. Warburton (L) | 1897-1898 |
| D. Farquharson (L) | 1898-1901 |
| A. Peters (L) | 1901-1908 |

| | |
|---|---|
| F.L. Haszard (L) | 1908-1911 |
| H. James Palmer (L) | 1911 |
| John. A. Mathieson (C) | 1911-1917 |
| Aubin E. Arsenault (C) | 1917-1919 |
| J.H. Bell (L) | 1919-1923 |
| James D. Stewart (C) | 1923-1927 |
| Albert C. Saunders (L) | 1927-1930 |
| Walter M. Lea (L) | 1930-1931 |
| James D. Stewart (C) | 1931-1933 |
| William J.P. MacMillan (C) | 1933-1935 |
| Walter M. Lea (L) | 1935-1936 |
| Thane M. Campbell (L) | 1936-1943 |
| J. Walter Jones (L) | 1943-1953 |
| Alexander W. Matheson (L) | 1953-1959 |
| Walter R. Shaw (C) | 1959-1966 |
| Alexander B. Campbell (L) | 1966-1978 |
| W. Bennett Campbell (L) | 1978-1979 |
| J. Angus MacLean (C) | 1979-1981 |
| James M. Lee (C) | 1981-present |

## Québec Administrations

| | |
|---|---|
| P.J. Chauveau (C) | 1867-1873 |
| G. Ouimet (C) | 1873-1874 |
| C.E.B. de Boucherville (C) | 1874-1878 |
| H.G. Joly (L) | 1878-1879 |
| J.A. Chapleau (C) | 1879-1882 |
| J.A. Mousseau (C) | 1882-1884 |
| J.J. Ross (C) | 1884-1887 |
| L.O. Taillon (C) | 1887 |
| H. Mercier (L) | 1887-1891 |
| C.E.B. de Boucherville (C) | 1891-1892 |

| | |
|---|---|
| L.O. Taillon (C) | 1892-1896 |
| E.J. Flynn (C) | 1896-1897 |
| F.G. Marchand (L) | 1897-1900 |
| S.N. Parent (L) | 1900-1905 |
| Sir L. Gouin (L) | 1905-1920 |
| Louis Alexandre Taschereau (L) | 1920-1936 |
| Adélard Godbout (L) | 1936 |
| Maurice Duplessis (UN) | 1936-1939 |
| J.A. Godbout (L) | 1939-1944 |
| Maurice Duplessis (UN) | 1944-1959 |
| J.P. Sauvé (UN) | 1959-1960 |
| Antonio Barrette (UN) | 1960 |
| Jean Lesage (L) | 1960-1966 |
| Daniel Johnson (UN) | 1966-1968 |
| J. Jacques Bertrand (UN) | 1968-1970 |
| Robert Bourassa (L) | 1970-1976 |
| René Lévesque (PQ) | 1976-present |

## Saskatchewan Administrations

| | |
|---|---|
| Walter Scott (L) | 1905-1916 |
| W.M. Martin (L) | 1916-1922 |
| C.A. Dunning (L) | 1922-1926 |
| James G. Gardiner (L) | 1926-1929 |
| J.T.M. Anderson (C) | 1929-1934 |
| James G. Gardiner (L) | 1934-1935 |
| William J. Paterson (L) | 1935-1944 |
| Thomas C. Douglas (CCF) | 1944-1961 |
| W.S. Lloyd (NDP-CCF) | 1961-1964 |
| W. Ross Thatcher (L) | 1964-1971 |
| A.E. Blakeney (NDP) | 1971-1982 |
| D. Grant Devine (C) | 1982-present |

# Provincial Elections Since 1967

## ALBERTA

| YEAR | DATE | PREMIER | PARTY | | LEADER OF OPPOSITION | | PARTY | OTHERS | TOTAL SEATS |
|------|------|---------|-------|----|------|----|-------|--------|-------------|
| 1967 | May 24 | Manning | SC | 55 | Lougheed | 6 | C | L-1;IND-1 | 65 |
| 1971 | Aug. 30 | Lougheed | C | 49 | Strom | 25 | SC | NDP-1 | 75 |
| 1975 | Mar. 26 | Lougheed** | C | 69 | Schmidt* | 4 | SC | NDP-1;IND-1 | 75 |
| 1979 | Mar. 14 | Lougheed | C | 74 | Clark | 4 | SC | NDP-1 | 79 |
| 1982 | Nov. 2 | Lougheed | C | 75 | Notley | 2 | NDP | IND-2 | 79 |

*Lost House seat.
**Record 62 percent of popular vote.

## BRITISH COLUMBIA

| YEAR | DATE | PREMIER | PARTY | | LEADER OF OPPOSITION | | PARTY | OTHERS | TOTAL SEATS |
|------|------|---------|-------|----|------|----|-------|--------|-------------|
| 1969 | Aug. 27 | W. Bennett | SC | 39 | Berger* | 11 | NDP | L-5 | 55 |
| 1972 | Aug. 30 | Barrett | NDP | 38 | W. Bennett | 10 | SC | L-5;C-2 | 55 |
| 1975 | Dec. 11 | W. Bennett | SC | 35 | Barrett* | 18 | NDP | L-1;C-1 | 55 |
| 1979 | May 10 | W. Bennett | SC | 31 | Barrett | 26 | NDP | | 56 |
| 1983 | May 6 | W. Bennett | SC | 35 | Barrett | 22 | NDP | | 51 |

*Lost House seat.

110

## MANITOBA

| YEAR | DATE | PREMIER | PARTY | LEADER OF OPPOSITION | PARTY | OTHERS | TOTAL SEATS |
|------|------|---------|-------|----------------------|-------|--------|-------------|
| 1969 | June 25 | Schreyer | NDP | Weir | 22 | C | L-5;SC-1;IND.-1 | 57 |
| 1973 | June 28 | Schreyer | 31 | NDP | Spivak | 21 | C | L-5 | 57 |
| 1977 | Oct. 11 | Lyon | 33 | C | Schreyer | 23 | NDP | L-1 | 57 |
| 1981 | Nov. 17 | Pawley | 34 | NDP | Lyon* | 23 | C | - | 57 |

*First Manitoba premier denied second term.

## NEW BRUNSWICK

| YEAR | DATE | PREMIER | PARTY | LEADER OF OPPOSITION | PARTY | OTHERS | TOTAL SEATS |
|------|------|---------|-------|----------------------|-------|--------|-------------|
| 1967 | Oct. 23 | Robichaud | 32 | L | Van Horne | 26 | C | - | 58 |
| 1970 | Oct. 26 | Hatfield | 31 | C | Robichaud | 27 | L | - | 58 |
| 1974 | Nov. 18 | Hatfield | 30 | C | Higgins | 25 | L | - | 58 |
| 1978 | Oct. 23 | Hatfield* | 30 | C | Daigle | 28 | L | - | 58 |
| 1982 | Oct. 12 | Hatfield | 39 | C | Young | 18 | L | NDP-1 | 58 |

*First Conservative premier to win three consecutive terms.

## NEWFOUNDLAND

| Year | Date | Premier | Seats | Party | Opponent | Seats | Party | Other | Total |
|---|---|---|---|---|---|---|---|---|---|
| 1971 | Oct. 28 | Moores** | 21 | C | Smallwood | 20 | L | NLP·1 | 42 |
| 1972 | Mar. 24 | Moores | 33 | C | Roberts | 9 | L | | 42 |
| 1975 | Sept. 16 | Moores | 30 | C | Roberts | 16 | L | LR·4;IND·1 | 51 |
| 1979 | June 18 | Peckford | 33 | C | Jamieson | 19 | L | ´ | 52 |
| 1982 | April 6 | Peckford | 44 | C | Stirling* | 8 | L | ´ | 52 |

*Lost House seat.
**First Conservative premier of Newfoundland.
Smallwood was Liberal premier from time Newfoundland joined Confederation (1949).

## NOVA SCOTIA

| Year | Date | Premier | Seats | Party | Opponent | Seats | Party | Other | Total |
|---|---|---|---|---|---|---|---|---|---|
| 1967 | May 30 | Stanfield | 40 | C | Regan | 6 | L | ´ | 46 |
| 1970 | Oct. 13 | Regan | 23 | L | Smith | 21 | C | NDP·2 | 46 |
| 1974 | April 2 | Regan | 31 | L | Buchanan | 12 | C | NDP·3 | 46 |
| 1978 | Sept. 19 | Buchanan | 31 | C | Regan | 17 | L | NDP·4 | 52 |
| 1981 | Oct. 6 | Buchanan | 37 | C | Cameron | 13 | L | NDP·1;IND·1 | 52 |

## ONTARIO

| YEAR | DATE | PREMIER | PARTY | LEADER OF OPPOSITION | | PARTY | OTHERS | TOTAL SEATS |
|---|---|---|---|---|---|---|---|---|
| 1967 | Oct. 17 | Robarts | C | 69 | Nixon 28 | L | NDP-20 | 117 |
| 1971 | Oct. 21 | Davis | C | 78 | Nixon 20 | L | NDP-19 | 117 |
| 1975 | Sept. 18 | Davis | C | 51 | Lewis 38 | NDP | L-36 | 125 |
| 1977 | June 9 | Davis | C | 58 | Smith 34 | L | NDP-33 | 125 |
| 1981 | Mar. 19 | Davis | C | 70 | Smith 34 | L | NDP-21 | 125 |

## PRINCE EDWARD ISLAND

| YEAR | DATE | PREMIER | PARTY | LEADER OF OPPOSITION | | PARTY | OTHERS | TOTAL SEATS |
|---|---|---|---|---|---|---|---|---|
| 1970 | May 11 | A. Campbell** | L | 27 | Key* 5 | C | ‘ | 32 |
| 1974 | Apr. 29 | A. Campbell | L | 26 | McQuaid 6 | C | ‘ | 32 |
| 1978 | Apr. 24 | A. Campbell | L | 17 | MacLean 15 | C | ‘ | 32 |
| 1979 | Apr. 23 | MacLean | C | 21 | B. Campbell 11 | L | ‘ | 32 |
| 1982 | Sept. 27 | Lee | C | 21 | Ghiz 11 | L | ‘ | 32 |

*Lost House seat.
**At thirty-two years of age youngest premier in Canada ever.

## QUEBEC

| Date | Winner | Seats | Party | Opposition | Seats | Party | Others | Total |
|---|---|---|---|---|---|---|---|---|
| 1970 Apr. 29 | Bourassa | 72 | L | Bertrand | 17 | UN | PQ-7;CR-12 | 108 |
| 1973 Oct. 29 | Bourassa** | 102 | L | Lévesque* | 6 | PQ | C-2 | 110 |
| 1976 Nov. 15 | Lévesque | 69 | PQ | Bourassa | 28 | L | UN-11; CR-1;PNP-1 | 110 |
| 1981 Apr. 13 | Lévesque | 80 | PQ | Ryan | 42 | L | - | 122 |

*Lost House seat.
**Greatest electoral victory in Québec history.

## SASKATCHEWAN

| Date | Winner | Seats | Party | Opposition | Seats | Party | Others | Total |
|---|---|---|---|---|---|---|---|---|
| 1967 Oct. 11 | Thatcher | 35 | L | Lloyd | 24 | CCF | - | 59 |
| 1971 June 23 | Blakeney | 45 | NDP | Thatcher | 15 | L | - | 60 |
| 1975 June 11 | Blakeney | 38 | L | Steuart | 15 | L | C-7;TE-1 | 61 |
| 1978 Oct. 18 | Blakeney | 44 | NDP | Collver | 17 | C | - | 61 |
| 1982 Apr. 26 | Devine | 57 | C | Blakeney | 7 | NDP | - | 64 |

## YUKON

| | | | | | | | | |
|---|---|---|---|---|---|---|---|---|
| 1978 Nov. 20 | Watson | 11 | C | MacKay | 2 | L | NDP-1;IND-2 | 16 |
| 1982 June 7 | Pearson | 9 | C | Plenikett | 6 | NDP | IND.-1 | 16 |

LEGEND:

C-Conservative  
L-Liberal  
PQ-Parti Québécois  
CR-Créditistes  
PNP-Parti Nationale Populaire  
UN-Union Nationale  

NDP-New Democratic Party  
SC-Social Credit  
IND.-Independent  
LR-Liberal Reform  
NLP-New Labour Party  
CCF-Co-operative Commonwealth Federation

# Twentieth-Century Provincial Parties Holding Office over Twenty Years

| PARTY | PREMIER | PROVINCE | DATES | YEARS |
|---|---|---|---|---|
| 1. Conservative | G.A. Drew | Ont. | 1943-1948 | |
| | T.L. Kennedy | | 1948-1949 | |
| | L. Frost | | 1949-1961 | |
| | J.P. Robarts | | 1961-1971 | |
| | W.G. Davis | | 1971-1984 | 40+ |
| 2. Liberal | F.G. Marchand | Qué. | 1897-1900* | |
| | S.N. Parent | | 1900-1905 | |
| | Sir L. Gouin | | 1905-1920 | |
| | L.A. Taschereau | | 1920-1936 | |
| | A. Godbout | | 1936 | 36+ |
| 3. Social Credit | W. Aberhart | Alta. | 1935-1943 | |
| | E.C. Manning | | 1943-1968 | |
| | H.E. Strom | | 1968-1971 | 36+ |
| 4. Liberal | W.T. Pipes | N.S. | 1882-1884* | |
| | W.S. Fielding | | 1884-1896* | |
| | G.H. Murray | | 1896-1923* | |
| | E.H. Armstrong | | 1923-1925 | 25+ |
| 5. Liberal | W. Scott | Sask. | 1905-1916 | |
| | W.M. Martin | | 1916-1922 | |
| | C.A. Dunning | | 1922-1926 | |
| | J.G. Gardiner | | 1926-1929 | 24+ |
| 6. Liberal | A.L. Macdonald | N.S. | 1933-1940 | |
| | A.S. MacMillan | | 1940-1945 | |
| | A.L. Macdonald | | 1945-1954 | |
| | H. Connolly | | 1954 | |
| | H.D. Hicks | | 1954-1956 | 23+ |
| 7. Liberal | J.R. Smallwood | Nfld. | 1949-1972 | 22+ |
| 8. United Farmers | J. Bracken | Man. | 1922-1943 | 20+ |
| 9. Social Credit | W.A.C. Bennett | B.C. | 1952-1972 | 20+ |

*Party took office before twentieth century.
  Total includes only years in office from 1900 onwards.

# Premiers over Ten Years in Office

| PREMIER | PARTY | PROVINCE | DATES IN OFFICE | YEARS IN OFFICE |
|---------|-------|----------|-----------------|-----------------|
| G.H. Murray | L | N.S. | 1896-1923 | 26+ |
| E.C. Manning | SC | Alta. | 1943-1968 | 25+ |
| O. Mowat | L | Ont. | 1872-1896 | 23+ |
| J.R. Smallwood | L | Nfld. | 1949-1972 | 22+ |
| J. Bracken | UF | Man. | 1922-1943 | 20+ |
| W.A.C. Bennett | SC | B.C. | 1952-1972 | 20+ |
| M. Duplessis | UN | Qué. | 1936-1939 1944-1959 | 18+ |
| T.C. Douglas | CCF | Sask. | 1944-1961 | 17+ |
| Sir L. Gouin | L | Qué. | 1905-1920 | 15+ |
| A.L. Macdonald | L | N.S. | 1933-1940 1945-1954 | 15+ |
| L.A. Taschereau | L | Qué. | 1920-1936 | 15+ |
| Sir R.P. Roblin | C | Man. | 1900-1915 | 15+ |
| R.B. Hatfield | C | N.B. | 1970-present | 13+ |
| A.G. Blair | L | N.B. | 1883-1896 | 13+ |
| E.P. Lougheed | C | Alta. | 1971-present | 12+ |
| J.B. McNair | L | N.B. | 1940-1952 | 12+ |
| R. McBride | C | B.C. | 1903-1915 | 12+ |
| L. Frost | C | Ont. | 1949-1961 | 12+ |
| W.G. Davis | C | Ont. | 1971-present | 12+ |
| A.B. Campbell | L | P.E.I. | 1966-1978 | 12+ |
| W.S. Fielding | L | N.S. | 1884-1896 | 11+ |
| T. Greenway | L | Man. | 1888-1900 | 11+ |
| A.E. Blakeney | NDP | Sask. | 1971-1982 | 11+ |
| L.J. Robichaud | L | N.B. | 1960-1970 | 10+ |
| R.L. Stanfield | C | N.S. | 1956-1967 | 10+ |
| J.W. Jones | L | P.E.I. | 1943-1953 | 10+ |

# SIX

# Comparative Statistical Data

Facts are most interesting or entertaining when they are compared with similar bits of information. What may seem trivial to one reader may fascinate another.

# Age

| | TOOK OFFICE | LEFT OFFICE | DIED |
|---|---|---|---|
| Macdonald | 52 | 76 | 76 |
| Mackenzie | 51 | 56 | 70 |
| Abbott | 70 | 71 | 72 |
| Thompson | 48 | 50 | 50 |
| Bowell | 70 | 72 | 93 |
| Tupper | 74 | 75 | 94 |
| Laurier | 55 | 70 | 77 |
| Borden | 57 | 66 | 82 |
| Meighen | 46 | 52 | 86 |
| King | 47 | 73 | 75 |
| Bennett | 60 | 65 | 76 |
| St. Laurent | 66 | 75 | 91 |
| Diefenbaker | 61 | 67 | 83 |
| Pearson | 65 | 70 | 74 |
| Trudeau | 48 | — | — |
| Clark | 39 | 40 | — |
| Average | 56.8 | 65.2 | 78.5 |

Average years alive after leaving office-11.5.

## Ambassadors
Pearson-United States (1945)

## Assassinations
None

# Authors

Mackenzie-*Speeches in Scotland and Canada* (1876)
*The Life and Speeches of George Brown* (1882)

Tupper-*Recollections of Sixty Years* (1914)

Borden-*Canadian Constitutional Studies* (1922)
*Canada in the Commonwealth* (1929)
*Robert Laird Borden: His Memoirs* (1938)

Meighen-*Overseas Addresses* (1921)
*The Greatest Englishman in History* (1936)
*Unrevised and Unrepented: Debating Speeches and Others* (1949)

King-*The Secret of Heroism* (1906)
*Industry and Humanity* (1918)
*The Message of the Carillon and other Addresses* (1927)
*Canada at Britain's Side* (1941)
*Canada and the Fight for Freedom* (1944)

Diefenbaker-*One Canada: The Crusading Years, 1895-1956* (1975)
*One Canada: The Years of Achievement, 1956-1962* (1976)
*One Canada: The Tumultuous Years, 1962-1967* (1977)

Pearson-*Democracy in World Politics* (1955)
*Diplomacy in the Nuclear Age* (1959)
*Mike-Vol. 1* (1972)
*Mike-Vol. 2* (1973)
*Mike-Vol. 3* (1975)

Trudeau-*La Grève de l'amiante* (1956)
*Deux innocents en Chine-rouge* (1961)

*The Future of Canadian Federalism* (1965)
*Politics: Canada* (1966)
*Réponses* (1967)
*Federalism and the French Canadians* (1968)
*Les Cheminements de la politique* (1970)
*Conversations with Canadians* (1972)

## Awards

Laurier-Star of Grand Officer of the Legion d'Honneur of France (1897)

Pearson-Order of the British Empire
Nobel Peace Prize (1957)

## Bachelors

King
Bennett

## Birthdates

Macdonald-January 11, 1815
Mackenzie-January 28, 1822
Abbott-March 12, 1821
Thompson-November 10, 1844
Bowell-December 27, 1823
Tupper-July 2, 1821
Laurier-November 2, 1841
Borden-June 26, 1854

Meighen-June 16, 1874
King-December 17, 1874
Bennett-July 3, 1870
St. Laurent-February 1, 1882
Diefenbaker-September 18, 1895
Pearson-April 23, 1897
Trudeau-October 18, 1919
Clark-June 5, 1939

## Birthplaces

Macdonald-Glasgow, Scotland
Mackenzie-Dunkeld, Scotland
Abbott-St. Andrews, Québec
Thompson-Halifax, Nova Scotia
Bowell-Rickinghall, England
Tupper-Amherst, Nova Scotia
Laurier-St. Lin, Québec
Borden-Grand Pré, Nova Scotia
Meighen-Anderson, Ontario

King-Berlin (Kitchener),
  Ontario
Bennett-Hopewell Hill,
  New Brunswick
St. Laurent-Compton, Québec
Diefenbaker-Neustadt, Ontario
Pearson-Newtonbrook, Ontario
Trudeau-Montréal, Québec
Clark-High River, Alberta

## Honorific Titles

Knight Commander of the Order of the Bath
    Macdonald (Victoria, 1867)
    Tupper (Victoria, 1879)
    Abbott (Victoria, 1892)
    Thompson (Victoria, 1894)
    Bowell (Victoria, 1895)
    Laurier (Victoria, 1897)

Knight Grand Cross of the Order of the Bath
    Macdonald (Victoria, 1884)

Knight Grand Cross of the Order of St. Michael and St. George
    Tupper (Victoria, 1886)
    Borden (George V, 1914)

Baronet of the United Kingdom
    Tupper (Victoria, 1888)

Viscount of Mickleham, Calgary, and Hopewell
    Bennett (George VI, 1941)

## Cabinet Positions Held

Macdonald
Minister of justice and attorney general (1867-73)
Minister of interior (1878-83)
Minister of railways and canals (1889-91)

Mackenzie
Minister of public works (1873-78)

Abbott
Minister without portfolio (1887-91)

Thompson
Minister of justice and attorney general (1885-94)

Bowell
Minister of customs (1878-92)
Minister of militia (1892)
Minister of trade and commerce (1892-94)

Tupper
Minister of inland revenue (1872-73)
Minister of customs (1873)
Minister of public works (1878-79)
Minister of railways and canals (1879-84)
Minister of finance (1887-88)
Secretary of state (1896)

Laurier
Minister of inland revenue (1877-78)

Borden
Secretary of state for external affairs (1912-20)

Meighen
Solicitor general (1915)
Secretary of state (1917)

Minister of the interior (1917)
Minister of mines (1919)
Secretary of state for external affairs (1920-21, 1926)
Minister without portfolio (1932-35)

King
Minister of labour (1909-11)
Secretary of state for external affairs (1921-26, 1935-46)

Bennett
Minister of justice (1921)
Minister of finance (1926)
Acting minister of the interior (1926)
Minister of mines (1926)
Secretary of state for external affairs (1930-35)

St. Laurent
Minister of justice and attorney general (1941-46)
Secretary of state for external affairs (1946-48)
Minister of justice (1948)

Diefenbaker
Secretary of state for external affairs (1957)

Pearson
Secretary of state for external affairs (1948-51)

Trudeau
Minister of justice and attorney general (1967)

## Children

| | | | |
|---|---|---|---|
| Macdonald-3 | Bowell-9 | Meighen-3 | Diefenbaker-0 |
| Mackenzie-3 | Tupper-6 | King-0 | Pearson-2 |
| Abbott-0 | Laurier-0 | Bennett-0 | Trudeau-3 |
| Thompson-5 | Borden-0 | St. Laurent-5 | Clark-1 |

## Death

DIED WHILE STILL MEMBERS OF PARLIAMENT

Macdonald (1891)        Laurier (1919)
Thompson (1894)        Diefenbaker (1979)
Mackenzie (1892)

DIED WHILE STILL PRIME MINISTER

Macdonald (1891)
Thompson (1894)

## Elections

NOT ELECTED AS PRIME MINISTER

Abbott          Bowell
Thompson        Tupper

NEVER HELD MAJORITY

Pearson (2 elections)
Clark (1 election)

ONLY PRIME MINISTER TO LOSE SEAT WHILE PARTY RETAINED POWER

King (1925, 1945)

CHOSEN BY CONVENTION

Liberals-King (1918)
           St. Laurent (1948)
           Pearson (1958)
           Trudeau (1968)
Conservatives-Bennett (1927)
           Diefenbaker (1956)
           Clark (1976)

MONTHS OF ELECTIONS (TOTAL 32)

| | | |
|---|---|---|
| January-1 | May-3 | September-3 |
| February-2 | June-7 | October-4 |
| March-3 | July-3 | November-3 |
| April-1 | August-2 | December-3 |

PARTY WINNING MOST SEATS WHILE LOSING POPULAR VOTE
   1896-Liberal   118 (45.1%), Conservative   88 (46.1%)
   1957-Conservative   112 (38.9%), Liberal   105 (40.9%)
   1979-Conservative   136 (36.0%), Liberal   114 (40.0%)

ONLY TIME MAJOR PARTY PLACED THIRD IN TOTAL SEATS
   1921-Conservatives 50 (Liberals-116, Progressives-64)

ONLY TIME PRIME MINISTERS FACED EACH OTHER IN SAME RIDING
   1926-King (E) and Diefenbaker (D) (Prince Albert, Sask.)

PARTY WINNING MOST BY-ELECTIONS
   1891-Conservative-27 seats

DEFEATED AS PRIME MINISTER BY VOTE IN HOUSE OF COMMONS
   Meighen (1926)
   Diefenbaker (1963)
   Clark (1980)

TOTAL PARTY YEARS IN OFFICE
   Liberals-69 years, 281 days (As of January 1, 1984)
      (King, Laurier, Trudeau, St. Laurent, Pearson and
      Mackenzie)
   Conservatives-49 years, 27 days
      (Macdonald, Borden, Diefenbaker, Bennett, Thompson,
      Meighen, Abbott, Bowell, Clark and Tupper)

LOST ELECTION AS INCUMBENT

| | | |
|---|---|---|
| Mackenzie-1878 | King-1925* | St. Laurent-1957 |
| Tupper-1896 | Meighen-1926 | Diefenbaker-1963 |
| Laurier-1911 | King-1930 | Trudeau-1979 |
| Meighen-1921 | Bennett-1935 | Clark-1980 |

*Liberals elected less seats than Conservatives, but King held onto prime ministership with help of minority parties.

PARTY WINNING ALL PROVINCIAL SEATS

Conservatives-B.C. (1872), B.C. (1874), B.C. (1878), B.C. (1882), B.C. (1887), B.C. (1891), B.C. (1904), B.C. (1911), P.E.I. (1957), Alta. (1958), Man. (1958), N.S. (1958), P.E.I. (1958), P.E.I. (1962), Sask. (1963), Sask. (1965), P.E.I. (1965), P.E.I. (1968), Alta. (1972), Alta. (1974), Alta. (1979), P.E.I. (1979), Alta. (1980).
TOTAL-23

Liberal-P.E.I. (1874), P.E.I. (1887), N.S. (1904), Qué. (1921), N.S. (1921), P.E.I. (1921), N.S. (1935), P.E.I. (1935), P.E.I. (1940), Nfld. (1953), Nfld. (1965).
TOTAL-12

Union-B.C. (1917), Sask. (1917)
TOTAL-2

LAST TIME MAJOR PARTY HAD OVER 50% OF POPULAR VOTE
Conservative-1958 (53.6%)
Liberal-1940 (51.5%)

GREATEST NUMBER OF SEATS
Conservatives-208 (1958)
Liberal-193 (1949)

LOWEST NUMBER OF SEATS
  Conservative-40 (1935, 1940)
  Liberal-49 (1958)

GREATEST PERCENT OF POPULAR VOTE*
  Conservative-53.6 (1958*)
  Liberal-52.0 (1904)

*Omitting Unionist government of 1917 (57.0%).

MAJORITY GOVERNMENTS
  Conservative-1867, 1872, 1878, 1882, 1887, 1891, 1911,
          1917, 1930, 1958
  Liberals-1874, 1896, 1900, 1904, 1908, 1935, 1940,
          1945, 1949, 1953, 1968, 1974, 1980

MINORITY GOVERNMENTS
  Conservatives-1957, 1962, 1979
  Liberals-1921, 1925, 1926, 1963, 1965, 1972

LOST FEDERAL ELECTIONS AS LEADER OF PARTY

| | | |
|---|---|---|
| Tupper | 1896, 1900 | 2 |
| Borden | 1904, 1908 | 2 |
| Laurier | 1911, 1917 | 2 |
| Meighen | 1920, 1926 | 2 |
| King | 1925,* 1930 | 2 |
| Diefenbaker | 1963, 1965 | 2 |
| Pearson | 1958, 1962 | 2 |
| Macdonald | 1874 | 1 |
| Mackenzie | 1878 | 1 |
| Bennett | 1935 | 1 |
| St. Laurent | 1957 | 1 |
| Trudeau | 1979 | 1 |
| Clark | 1980 | 1 |

*Lost election, retained prime ministership.

FEDERAL ELECTIONS WON (PARTY TOTALS)
  Liberals-18
  Conservatives-14

WON FEDERAL ELECTION AS LEADER OF PARTY
  Macdonald-6 (1867, 1872, 1878, 1882, 1887, 1891)
  King-5 (1920, 1926, 1935, 1940, 1945)
  Trudeau-4 (1968, 1972, 1974, 1980)
  Laurier-4 (1896, 1900, 1904, 1908)
  Diefenbaker-3 (1957, 1958, 1962)
  Borden-2 (1911, 1917)
  St. Laurent-2 (1949, 1953)
  Pearson-2 (1963, 1965)
  Mackenzie-1 (1874)
  Meighen-1 (1925)*
  Bennett-1 (1930)
  Clark-1 (1979)

*Won election with minority of seats; King retained prime ministership.

RAN IN MOST GENERAL ELECTIONS
  Diefenbaker-15

RAN IN LEAST GENERAL ELECTIONS
  Thompson-2

WON MOST GENERAL ELECTIONS
  Diefenbaker-13

LOST MOST GENERAL ELECTIONS
  King-4

WON MOST BY-ELECTIONS
  Tupper-4

LOST MOST BY-ELECTIONS

  Laurier-1          Meighen-1

AGE ENTERING HOUSE OF COMMONS

| | | |
|---|---|---|
| Macdonald-52 | Laurier-32 | Diefenbaker-44 |
| Mackenzie-45 | Borden-32 | Pearson-50 |
| Abbott-46 | Meighen-34 | Trudeau-46 |
| Thompson-41 | King-34 | Clark-33 |
| Bowell-43 | Bennett-41 | |
| Tupper-46 | St. Laurent-59 | |

# Fathers of Confederation

LAST SURVIVOR OF FATHERS OF CONFEDERATION

Tupper

FATHERS OF CONFEDERATION WHO BECAME PRIME MINISTER

Macdonald            Tupper

# Lawyers

| | | | |
|---|---|---|---|
| Macdonald | 1836 (Ont.)* | Bennett | 1893 (N.S.) |
| Thompson | 1865 (N.S.) | Meighen | 1902 (Man.) |
| | 1890 (Ont.) | St. Laurent | 1905 (Qué.) |
| Laurier | 1865 (Qué.) | Diefenbaker | 1919 (Sask.) |
| Abbott | 1877 (Qué.) | Trudeau | 1943 (Qué.) |
| Borden | 1878 (N.S.) | | |

*Date admitted to bar.

# Longest-Shortest

LONGEST TIME IN OFFICE

King-21 years, 49 days

LONGEST CONSECUTIVE YEARS IN OFFICE
Laurier-15 years

SHORTEST TIME IN OFFICE
Tupper-68 days

LONGEST TERM IN OFFICE BY COMMONWEALTH PRIME MINISTER
King

## Marriages

MARRIED MORE THAN ONCE
Macdonald-Twice      Diefenbaker-Twice
Mackenzie-Twice

FIRST MARRIED WHEN PRIME MINISTER
Trudeau (1971)

OLDEST WHEN MARRIED FOR THE FIRST TIME
Trudeau-51

OLDEST WHEN MARRIED FOR THE SECOND TIME
Diefenbaker-58

## Military Service

Mackenzie-Major, Twenty-seventh Lambton Battalion Volunteer Infantry (1866-74)

Abbott-Commanded Argenteuil Rangers (1866)

Bowell-Major, Forty-ninth Hastings Battalion of Militia (1867-72)

Diefenbaker-Lieutenant, World War I

Pearson-Private, lieutenant, and flying officer (1915-18)

## Miscellaneous

SCHOOL TEACHERS
   Borden      Bennett

PROFESSORS OR LECTURERS
   St. Laurent
   Pearson
   Trudeau
   Clark

DIED IN ONE DECADE
1890s (4)
   Macdonald (1891); Mackenzie (1892); Abbott (1893);
   Thompson (1894)

1970s (3)
   Pearson (1972); St. Laurent (1973); Diefenbaker (1979)

## Millionaires

   Bennett      Trudeau

## Money

APPEAR ON CURRENCY (PAPER)
   Laurier-$5        King-$50
   Macdonald-$10     Borden-$100

## Prime Ministers

RESIGNED AS PRIME MINISTER
   Macdonald (1873)      Succeeded by Mackenzie*
   Abbott (1892)         Succeeded by Thompson
   Bowell (1896)         Succeeded by Tupper

132

| Borden (1920) | Succeeded by Meighen |
| King (1926) | Succeeded by Meighen* |
| King (1948) | Succeeded by St. Laurent |
| Pearson (1968) | Succeeded by Trudeau |
| Trudeau (1984) | |

*Opposition leader.

FIRST PRIME MINISTER BORN IN NINETEENTH CENTURY
Macdonald (1815)

LAST PRIME MINISTER BORN IN NINETEENTH CENTURY
Pearson (1897)

FIRST PRIME MINISTER BORN IN TWENTIETH CENTURY
Trudeau (1919)

PHYSICIAN
Tupper

PRIME MINISTER WITH NO FORMER PRIME MINISTERS ALIVE DURING ANY PART OF TERM
2-Macdonald, Bowell

PRIME MINISTERS WITH NO FORMER PRIME MINISTERS ALIVE DURING SOME PART OF TERM
4-Macdonald, Abbott, Thompson, Bowell

PRIME MINISTER WITH ONLY ONE FORMER PRIME MINISTER ALIVE DURING ALL OF TERM
3-Mackenzie (Macdonald), Tupper (Bowell), Meighen (Borden)

PRIME MINISTER WITH MOST FORMER PRIME MINISTERS ALIVE DURING ALL OF TERM
3-Bennett (Borden, Meighen, King)

PRIME MINISTERS WITH MOST FORMER PRIME MINISTERS ALIVE
DURING ANY PART OF TERM
3-Borden (Bowell, Tupper, Laurier)
3-Bennett (Borden, Meighen, King)
4-Trudeau (St. Laurent, Diefenbaker, Pearson, Clark)

BORN OUTSIDE CANADA
Macdonald-Glasgow, Scotland
Mackenzie-Dunkeld, Scotland
Bowell-Rickinghall, England

FIRST NATIVE BORN
Abbott-St. Andrews, Québec

NEVER TO MEET PARLIAMENT WHILE PRIME MINISTER
Tupper

WON NOBEL PRIZE
Pearson (Peace, 1957)

LONGEST SESSION OF PARLIAMENT
30th Session-Sept. 30, 1974 to July 30, 1976

FIRST CHILD BORN TO PRIME MINISTER IN OFFICE
Mary-Macdonald

SECOND CHILD BORN TO PRIME MINISTER IN OFFICE
Justin-Trudeau

FIRST TO TRAVEL OUTSIDE CANADA AS PRIME MINISTER
Macdonald-Washington (1871)

FIRST OPENING OF PARLIAMENT BROADCAST ON TELEVISION
1955

FIRST CAMPAIGN RADIO BROADCAST
1930

JUDGE
Thompson-Puisne judge of Supreme Court of Nova Scotia (1882-85)

SENATORS
Abbott*      Bowell*      Meighen
*While prime minister.

OLDEST PRIME MINISTER WHEN FIRST TAKING OFFICE
Tupper-74

YOUNGEST PRIME MINISTER WHEN FIRST TAKING OFFICE
Clark-39

ONLY PRIME MINISTER BURIED OUTSIDE CANADA
Bennett-England

YOUNGEST PRIME MINISTER TO DIE
Thompson-50

FIRST SERVED IN MILITARY OVERSEAS
Diefenbaker

FIRST HONORIFIC TITLE HOLDER
Macdonald (K.C.B., G.C.B.)

LAST HONORIFIC TITLE HOLDER
Bennett (Viscount)

PRIME MINISTERS WHO HAD SONS WHO BECAME MEMBERS OF PARLIAMENT
Macdonald      Tupper      St. Laurent

FIRST HELD OFFICE BY DEFAULT, DEATH, OR RESIGNATION
Mackenzie (1873)      Tupper (1896)
Abbott (1891)         Meighen (1919)
Thompson (1892)       St. Laurent (1948)
Bowell (1894)         Trudeau (1968)

POLITICAL PARTY

| Macdonald | Conservative |
| Mackenzie | Liberal |
| Abbott | Conservative |
| Thompson | Conservative |
| Bowell | Conservative |
| Tupper | Conservative |
| Laurier | Liberal |
| Borden | Conservative |
| Meighen | Conservative |
| King | Liberal |
| Bennett | Conservative |
| St. Laurent | Liberal |
| Diefenbaker | Conservative |
| Pearson | Liberal |
| Trudeau | Liberal |
| Clark | Conservative |

TOTAL

Conservative 10     Liberal 6

TIME IN OFFICE

| King | 21 years | 49 days |
| Macdonald | 18 years | 359 days |
| Trudeau* | 15 years | 115 days |
| Laurier | 15 years | 88 days |
| Borden | 8 years | 273 days |
| St. Laurent | 8 years | 218 days |
| Diefenbaker | 5 years | 236 days |
| Bennett | 5 years | 77 days |
| Pearson | 4 years | 363 days |
| Mackenzie | 4 years | 343 days |

| Thompson | 2 years | 7 days |
| Meighen | 1 year | 261 days |
| Abbott | 1 year | 171 days |
| Bowell | 1 year | 127 days |
| Clark | 0 years | 273 days |
| Tupper | 0 years | 68 days |

*As of April 30, 1984.

OCCUPATION AFTER PRIME MINISTER
Macdonald-Died in office
Mackenzie-Member of Parliament
Abbott-Retired
Thompson-Died in office
Bowell-Senator
Laurier-Member of Parliament
Borden-Diplomat
Meighen-Senator
King-Retired
Bennett-House of Lords
St. Laurent-Lawyer
Diefenbaker-Member of Parliament
Pearson-Author
Trudeau-Present prime minister
Clark-Member of Parliament

RE-ELECTED PRIME MINISTER AFTER LOSING OFFICE
| Macdonald | 1878 |
| King | 1926, 1935 |
| Trudeau | 1980 |

PRIME MINISTER FOR NON-CONSECUTIVE TERMS
| Macdonald | King |
| Meighen | Trudeau |

# Privy Council

| | | | |
|---|---|---|---|
| Macdonald | 1867 | Borden | 1911 |
| Tupper | 1870 | Meighen | 1915 |
| Mackenzie | 1873 | Bennett | 1921 |
| Laurier | 1877 | St. Laurent | 1941 |
| Bowell | 1878 | Diefenbaker | 1957 |
| Thompson | 1885 | Pearson | 1948 |
| Abbott | 1887 | Trudeau | 1967 |
| King | 1909 | Clark | 1979 |

| | | | |
|---|---|---|---|
| Macdonald | 1872 | King | 1922 |
| Thompson | 1888 | Bennett | 1930 |
| Laurier | 1897 | St. Laurent | 1946 |
| Tupper | 1907 | Diefenbaker | 1957 |
| Borden | 1912 | Pearson | 1963 |
| Meighen | 1920 | | |

# Provinces

| | | | |
|---|---|---|---|
| Macdonald | Ontario | Meighen | Ontario |
| Mackenzie | Ontario | King | Ontario |
| Abbott | Ontario | Bennett | Alberta |
| Thompson | Nova Scotia | St. Laurent | Québec |
| Bowell | Ontario | Diefenbaker | Saskatchewan |
| Tupper | Nova Scotia | Pearson | Ontario |
| Laurier | Québec | Trudeau | Québec |
| Borden | Nova Scotia | Clark | Alberta |

BORN IN PROVINCE OTHER THAN THE PROVINCE REPRESENTED
Bennett     New Brunswick     Diefenbaker     Ontario

## Provincial Government Positions

Macdonald (Canada West: Ontario)
    M.L.A. (1844-67)
    Receiver general (1847)
    Commissioner of crown lands (1847-48)
    Attorney general (1854-58)
    Postmaster general (1858-62, 1864-67)
    Minister of militia affairs (1862-65)

Mackenzie (Canada West: Ontario)
    M.L.A. (1861-67, 71)
    Member of executive council (1871)

Abbott (Canada East: Québec)
    M.L.A. (1857-67)
    Mayor of Montréal (1887-88)
    Solicitor general (1862-63)

Thompson (Nova Scotia)
    M.L.A. (1877-82)
    Executive council and attorney general (1878-82)
    Premier (1882)

Tupper (Nova Scotia)
    M.L.A. (1855-57, 1857-67)
    Provincial secretary (1857-60, 1863-67)
    Premier (1864-67)

Laurier (Québec)
    M.L.A. (1871-74)

Bennett (Alberta)
  M.L.A. (1909-11)

Diefenbaker (Saskatchewan)
  Leader of Conservative party (1936-38)

## Premiers

PREMIERS
  Tupper-Nova Scotia
  Thompson-Nova Scotia

## World Government

PARIS PEACE CONFERENCE (1919)
  Borden-Chief Canadian delegate

LEAGUE OF NATIONS
  Borden-Chairman, Sixth Committee of the Assembly (1930)
  King-Vice-president of the Assembly (1928, 1936)
  Bennett-Canadian delegate (1934)

UNITED NATIONS
  King-Chairman, Canadian delegation to San Francisco
        Conferences (1945)
        Paris Conference (1946)
        General Assembly (1948)
  Pearson-President of General Assembly (1952-53)

# SEVEN

# Lists and Charts

# Fathers of Confederation
# Charlottetown Conference (September 1864)

## CANADA (QUEBEC AND ONTARIO)

Sir John Alexander Macdonald-Premier of Province of Canada
Sir George-Etienne Cartier-Legislator
Sir Alexander Tilloch Galt-Legislator
William McDougall-Legislator
Sir Hector-Louis Langevin-Legislator
George Brown-Legislator
Thomas D'Arcy McGee*-Legislator
Sir Alexander Campbell-Legislative Council
*Only member of Parliament ever assassinated (1868).

## NOVA SCOTIA

Sir Charles Hibbert Tupper-Premier of Nova Scotia
William Alexander Henry-Legislator
Jonathan McCully-Journalist
Sir Adams George Archibald-Legislator

## NEW BRUNSWICK

Sir Samuel Leonard Tilley-Premier of New Brunswick
John Mercer Johnson-Legislator
William Henry Steeves-Legislator
Edward Baron Chandler-Legislator
John Hamilton Gray-Legislator

## PRINCE EDWARD ISLAND

John Hamilton Gray-Premier of Prince Edward Island
Edward Palmer-Legislative Council
William Henry Pope-Legislator
Andrew Archibald Macdonald-Legislator
George Coles-Leader of opposition

# Québec Conference (October 1864)

## CANADA (QUEBEC AND ONTARIO)

Sir John Alexander Macdonald-Premier of Province of Canada
Sir George-Etienne Cartier-Legislator
Sir Alexander Tilloch Galt-Legislator
William McDougall-Legislator
Sir Hector-Louis Langevin-Legislator
George Brown-Legislator
Thomas D'Arcy McGee-Legislator
Sir Alexander Campbell-Legislative Council
Sir Etienne Paschal Taché-Legislator (died 1865)
Sir Oliver Mowat-Legislator
Jean-Charles Chapais-Legislator
James Cockburn-Legislator

## NOVA SCOTIA

Sir Charles Hibbert Tupper-Premier of Nova Scotia
William Alexander Henry-Legislator
Jonathan McCully-Journalist
Sir Adams George Archibald-Legislator
Robert Barry Dickey-Legislative Council

## NEW BRUNSWICK

Samuel Leonard Tilley-Premier of New Brunswick
John Mercer Johnson-Legislator
William Henry Steeves-Legislator
Edward Baron Chandler-Legislator
John Hamilton Gray-Legislator
Peter Mitchell-Legislator
Charles Fisher-Legislator

## PRINCE EDWARD ISLAND

John Hamilton Gray-Premier of Prince Edward Island
Edward Palmer-Legislative Council
William H. Opoe-Legislator
Andrew Archibald MacDonald-Legislator
George Coles-Leader of opposition
Thomas Heath Haviland-Legislator
Edward Whelan-Legislative Council

## NEWFOUNDLAND

Sir Frederick Bowker Terrington Carter-Legislator
Sir Ambrose Shea-Legislator

# London Conference (December 1866)

## CANADA (QUEBEC AND ONTARIO)

Sir John Alexander Macdonald-Premier of Province of Canada
Sir George-Etienne Cartier-Legislator

Sir Alexander Tilloch Galt-Legislator
William McDougall-Legislator
Sir Hector-Louis Langevin-Legislator
Sir William Pierce Howland-Legislator

## NOVA SCOTIA

Sir Charles Hibbert Tupper-Premier of Nova Scotia
William Alexander Henry-Legislator
Jonathan McCully-Journalist
Sir Adams George Archibald-Legislator
John William Ritchie-Legislative Council, senator

## NEW BRUNSWICK

Sir Samuel Leonard Tilley-Premier of New Brunswick
John Mercer Johnson-Legislator
Peter Mitchell-Legislator
Charles Fisher-Legislator
Robert Duncan Wilmot-Legislator

# Governors General of Canada

| NAME | DATE TOOK OFFICE |
|------|------------------|
| The Rt. Hon. The Viscount Monck | 1867 |
| The Rt. Hon. The Lord Lisgar | 1869 |
| The Rt. Hon. The Earl of Dufferin | 1872 |
| The Most Hon. The Marquess of Lorne | 1878 |
| The Most Hon. The Marquess of Lansdowne | 1883 |

| | |
|---|---|
| The Rt. Hon. The Lord Stanley of Preston | 1888 |
| The Rt. Hon. The Earl of Aberdeen | 1893 |
| The Rt. Hon. The Earl of Minto | 1898 |
| The Rt. Hon. The Earl Grey | 1904 |
| Field Marshall H.R.H. The Duke of Connaught and of Strathearn | 1911 |
| The Rt. Hon. The Duke of Devonshire | 1916 |
| General The Rt. Hon. The Lord Byng of Vimy | 1921 |
| The Rt. Hon. The Viscount Willingdon | 1926 |
| The Rt. Hon. The Earl of Bessborough | 1931 |
| The Rt. Hon. The Lord Tweedsmuir | 1935 |
| The Rt. Hon. The Earl of Athlone | 1940 |
| Field Marshall The Rt. Hon. The Viscount Alexander of Tunis | 1946 |
| The Rt. Hon. Vincent Massey* | 1952 |
| General The Rt. Hon. George Philias Vanier | 1959 |
| The Rt. Hon. Roland Michener | 1967 |
| The Rt. Hon. Jules Léger | 1974 |
| The Rt. Hon. Edward Richard Schreyer | 1979 |
| The Rt. Hon. Jeanne Sauvé** | 1984 |

*First Canadian-born governor general.
**First woman governor general.

## Speakers of the Senate

| | |
|---|---|
| Joseph Edouard Cauchon | 1867-69 |
| John Ross | 1869 |
| Joseph Edouard Cauchon | 1869-1872 |
| Amos Edwin Botsford | 1872 |
| Joseph Edouard Cauchon | 1872 |

| | |
|---|---|
| Pierre J.O. Chauveau | 1873-74 |
| David Christie | 1874-78 |
| Robert Duncan Wilmot | 1878-80 |
| David Lewis Macpherson | 1880 |
| Amos Edwin Boysford | 1880 |
| David Lewis Macpherson | 1880-83 |
| William Miller | 1883-87 |
| Joseph Burr Plumb | 1887-88 |
| George William Allan | 1888-91 |
| Alexandre Lacoste | 1891 |
| John Jones Ross | 1891-96 |
| Charles Alphonse P. Pelletier | 1896-1901 |
| Lawrence Geoffrey Power | 1901-05 |
| Raoul Dandurand | 1905-09 |
| James Kirkpatrick Kerr | 1909-11 |
| Aug. Chs. Philippe Robert Landry | 1911-16 |
| Joseph Bolduc | 1916-22 |
| Hewitt Bostock | 1922-30 |
| Arthur Charles Hardy | 1930 |
| Pierre Edouard Blondin | 1930-36 |
| Walter Edward Foster | 1936-40 |
| Georges Parent | 1940-42 |
| Thomas Vien | 1943-45 |
| James Horace King | 1945-49 |
| Elie Beauregard | 1949-53 |
| Wishart MacLea Robertson | 1953-57 |
| Mark Robert Drouin | 1957-62 |
| George Stanley White | 1962-63 |
| Maurice Bourget | 1963-66 |
| Sydney John Smith | 1966-68 |
| Jean-Paul Deschatelets | 1968-72 |

| | |
|---|---|
| Muriel McQueen Fergusson* | 1972-74 |
| L.M. Renaude Lapointe | 1974-79 |
| Allister Grosart | 1979-80 |
| Jean Marchand | 1980-present |

*First woman speaker of the Senate.

## Speakers of the House of Commons

| | |
|---|---|
| James Cockburn | 1867-74 |
| Timothy Warren Anglin | 1874-77, 1878-79 |
| Joseph-Goderic Blanchet | 1879-83 |
| George Airey Kirkpatrick | 1883-87 |
| Joseph Aldéric Quimet | 1887-91 |
| Peter White | 1891-96 |
| Sir James David Edgar | 1896-99 |
| Thomas Bain | 1899-1901 |
| Louis Phillippe Brodeur | 1901-04 |
| Napoleon Antoine Belcourt | 1904-05 |
| Robert Franklin Sutherland | 1905-09 |
| Charles Marcil | 1909-11 |
| Thomas Simpson Sproule | 1911-15 |
| Albert Sévigny | 1916-17 |
| Edgar Nelson Rhodes | 1917-22 |
| Rodolphe Lemieux | 1922-30 |
| George Black | 1930-35 |
| James Langstaff Bowman | 1935-36 |
| Pierre François Casgrain | 1936-40 |
| James Allison Glen | 1940-45 |
| Gaspard Fauteux | 1945-49 |
| William Ross Macdonald | 1949-53 |

| Louis René Beaudoin | 1953-57 |
| Daniel Roland Michener | 1957-62 |
| Marcel-Joseph-Aimé Lambert | 1962 |
| Alan A. Macnaughton | 1963-66 |
| Lucien Lamoureux | 1966-74 |
| James A. Jerome | 1974-79 |
| Jeanne Sauvé* | 1979-83 |
| Lloyd Francis | 1983-present |

*First woman speaker of House of Commons.

# Present* Federal Cabinet

| Prime minister | Pierre Elliott Trudeau |
| Minister of state (Canadian Wheat Board) | Hazen Robert Argue |
| Minister of state for social development | Jacob (Jack) Austin |
| Transport | Lloyd Axworthy |
| National health and welfare | Monique Bégin |
| National defence | Jean-Jacques Blais |
| National revenue | Pierre Bussières |
| Environment | Charles L. Caccia |
| Veterans' affairs | W. Bennett Campbell |
| Energy, mines and resources | Joseph-Jacques Jean Chrétien |
| Minister of state (multiculturalism) | David Michael Collenette |
| Fisheries and oceans | Pierre de Bané |

| | |
|---|---|
| Consumer and corporate affairs; minister responsible for status of women | Judith A. Erola |
| Communications | Francis Fox |
| President of Treasury Board | Herbert E. Gray |
| Minister of state (fitness and amateur sport) | Céline Hervieux-Payette |
| Minister of state for economic development; minister of state for science and technology | Donald James Johnston |
| Secretary of state | Serge Joyal |
| Solicitor general | Robert Phillip Kaplan |
| Finance | Marc Lalonde |
| Supply and services; receiver general for Canada | Charles Lapointe |
| Public works with responsibility for C.M.H.C. and N.C.C. | Roméo A. LeBlanc |
| Industry, trade and commerce; regional economic expansion | Edward Lumley |
| Deputy prime minister; secretary of state for external affairs | Allan J. MacEachen |
| Justice; attorney general for Canada | Mark R. MacGuigan |
| Minister of state (finance) | Roy MacLaren |
| Indian affairs and northern development | John Carr Munro |

| | |
|---|---|
| Leader of the government in Senate | Horace Andrew (Bud) Olson |
| Labour; minister responsible for the Canada Post Corporation | André Ouellet |
| Minister of state (external relations) | Jean-Luc Pepin |
| President of the Privy Council; government House leader | Yvon Pinard |
| Minister of state (international trade) | Gerald Augustine Regan |
| Employment and immigration | John Roberts |
| Minister of state (small businesses and tourism) | David Paul Smith |
| Agriculture | Eugene Francis Whelan |

*As of November 1, 1983.

# Governments Since Confederation

Macdonald (Conservative)-July 1, 1867-Nov. 6, 1873
Mackenzie (Liberal)-Nov. 7, 1873-Oct. 16, 1878
Macdonald (Conservative)-Oct. 17, 1878-June 6, 1891
Abbott (Conservative)-June 16, 1891-Dec. 5, 1892
Thompson (Conservative)-Dec. 5, 1892-Dec. 12, 1892
Bowell (Conservative)-Dec. 21, 1894-April 27, 1896
Tupper (Conservative)-May 1, 1896-July 8, 1896
Laurier (Liberal)-July 11, 1896-Oct. 6, 1911
Borden (Conservative)-Oct. 10, 1911-Oct. 12, 1917

Borden (Unionist)-Oct. 10, 1911-July 10, 1920

Meighen (Unionist-National Liberal and Conservative party)-
 July 10, 1920-Dec. 29, 1921

King (Liberal)-Dec. 29, 1921-June 28, 1926

Meighen, (Conservative)-June 28, 1926-Sept. 25, 1926

King (Liberal)-Sept. 25, 1926-Aug. 7, 1930

Bennett (Conservative)-Aug. 7, 1930-Oct. 23, 1935

King (Liberal)-Oct. 23, 1935-Nov. 15, 1948

St. Laurent (Liberal)-Nov. 15, 1948-June 21, 1957

Diefenbaker (Conservative)-June 21, 1957-April 22, 1963

Pearson (Liberal)-April 22, 1963-April 20, 1968

Trudeau (Liberal)-April 20, 1968-June 4, 1979

Clark (Conservative)-June 4, 1979-March 3, 1980

Trudeau (Liberal)-March 3, 1980-present

# Chief Justices of the Supreme Court

|  | TERM |
|---|---|
| Sir William Buell Richard | 1875-1879 |
| Sir William Johnston Ritchie | 1879-1892 |
| Sir Samuel Henry Strong | 1892-1902 |
| Sir Henri Elzéar Taschereau | 1902-1906 |
| Sir Charles Fitzpatrick | 1906-1918 |
| Sir Louis Henry Davies | 1918-1924 |
| Francis Alexander Anglin | 1924-1933 |
| Sir Lyman Poore Duff | 1933-1944 |
| Thibaudeau Rinfret | 1944-1954 |
| Patrick Kerwin | 1954-1963 |
| Robert Taschereau | 1963-1967 |
| J.R. Cartwright | 1967-1970 |

| | |
|---|---|
| Gérald Fauteaux | 1970-1973 |
| Bora Laskin | 1973-1984 |
| Brian Dickson | 1984- |

# Present Justices of the Supreme Court

## CHIEF JUSTICE OF CANADA    APPOINTED

| | |
|---|---|
| Brian Dickson | April 18, 1984 |

## PUISNE JUDGES

| | |
|---|---|
| Roland Almon Ritchie | May 5, 1959 |
| R.G. Brian Dickson | March 26, 1973 |
| Jean Beetz | January 1, 1974 |
| Willard Zebedee Estey | September 29, 1977 |
| William R. McIntyre | January 1, 1979 |
| Julien Chouinard | September 24, 1979 |
| Antonio Lamer | March 18, 1980 |
| Bertha Wilson | March 4, 1982 |

Conventions

## CONSERVATIVE

| DATE | PLACE | WINNER | PROVINCE | POSITION | OTHER CANDIDATES | BALLOT |
|------|-------|--------|----------|----------|------------------|--------|
| 1927 | Winnipeg, Man. | R.B. Bennett | Alta. | M.P. | 6 | Second |
| 1938 | Ottawa, Ont. | R.J. Manion | Ont. | Former M.P. | 5 | Second |
| 1942 | Winnipeg, Man. | J. Bracken | Man. | Premier | 5 | Second |
| 1948 | Ottawa, Ont. | G. Drew | Ont. | Premier | 3 | First |
| 1956 | Ottawa, Ont. | J. Diefenbaker | Sask. | M.P. | 3 | First |
| 1967 | Toronto, Ont. | R. Stanfield | N.S. | Premier | 11 | Fifth |
| 1976 | Ottawa, Ont. | J. Clark | Alta. | M.P. | 11 | Fourth |

## LIBERAL

| DATE | PLACE | WINNER | PROVINCE | POSITION | OTHER CANDIDATES | BALLOT |
|------|-------|--------|----------|----------|------------------|--------|
| 1919 | Ottawa, Ont. | W.L.M. King | Ont. | Former M.P. | 4 | Fifth |
| 1948 | Ottawa, Ont. | L. St. Laurent | Qué. | M.P. | 3 | First |
| 1958 | Ottawa, Ont. | L. Pearson | Ont. | M.P. | 3 | First |

## Conservative Leadership Convention Ottawa-June 10-12, 1983

| CANDIDATES | PROVINCE | POSITION | BALLOTS | | | |
|---|---|---|---|---|---|---|
| | | | 1 | 2 | 3 | 4 |
| Mulroney | Qué. | Lawyer | 874 | 1021 | 1036 | 1584 |
| Clark | Alta. | M.P. | 1091 | 1085 | 1058 | 1325 |
| Crosbie | Nfld. | M.P. | 639 | 781 | 858 | |
| Crombie | Ont. | M.P. | 116 | 67 | | |
| Wilson | Ont. | M.P. | 144 | | | |
| Pocklington | Alta. | Businessman | 102 | | | |
| Gamble | Ont. | M.P. | 17 | | | |
| Fraser | Ont. | Businessman | 5 | | | |
| TOTAL | | | 2988 | 2954 | 2952 | 2909 |

## Liberal Leadership Convention Ottawa-April 4-6, 1968

| CANDIDATES | PROVINCE | POSITION | 1 | BALLOTS 2 | 3 | 4 |
|---|---|---|---|---|---|---|
| Trudeau | Qué. | M.P. | 732 | 964 | 1051 | 1203 |
| Hellyer | Ont. | M.P. | 330 | 465 | 377 | |
| Winters | N.S. | M.P. | 293 | 473 | 621 | 954 |
| Turner | Ont. | M.P. | 277 | 347 | 279 | 195 |
| Martin | Ont. | M.P. | 277 | | | |
| Greene | Ont. | M.P. | 169 | 104 | 29 | |
| MacEachen | N.S. | M.P. | 165 | 11 | | |
| Kierans | Qué. | M.L.A. | 103 | | | |
| TOTAL | | | 2366 | 2364 | 2357 | 2352 |

## PROVINCIAL GOVERNMENTS, CONFEDERATION TO THE PRESENT

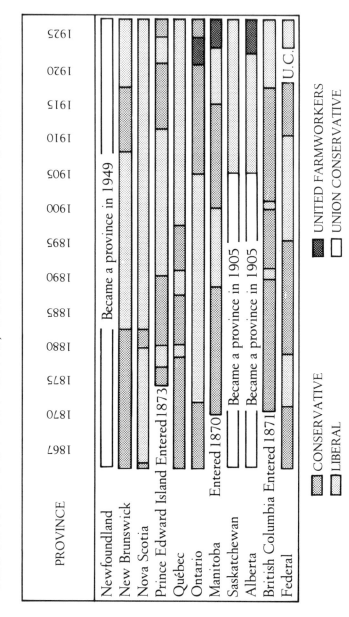

| PROVINCE | 1867 | 1870 | 1875 | 1880 | 1885 | 1890 | 1895 | 1900 | 1905 | 1910 | 1915 | 1920 | 1925 |
|---|---|---|---|---|---|---|---|---|---|---|---|---|---|

Newfoundland — Became a province in 1949

New Brunswick

Nova Scotia

Prince Edward Island Entered 1873

Québec

Ontario

Manitoba Entered 1870

Saskatchewan — Became a province in 1905

Alberta — Became a province in 1905

British Columbia Entered 1871

Federal

U.C.

CONSERVATIVE · LIBERAL · UNITED FARMWORKERS · UNION CONSERVATIVE

# PROVINCIAL GOVERNMENTS, CONFEDERATION TO THE PRESENT
## (CONTINUED)

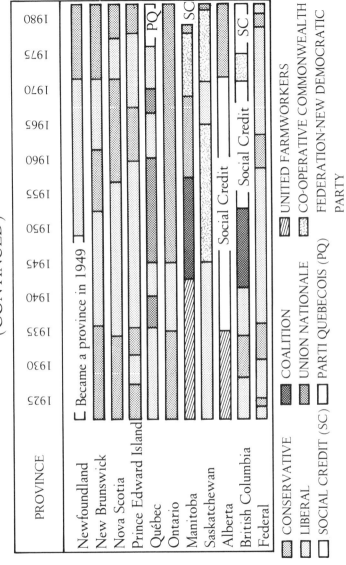

# CANADA AND WORLD LEADERS

| YEAR | PRIME MINISTER | GOVERNOR GENERAL* | U.S. PRESIDENT | MONARCH | U.K. PRIME MINISTER |
|---|---|---|---|---|---|
| 1867 | Macdonald | Monck | Johnson | Victoria | Earl of Derby |
| 1869 | | Lisgar | | | Disraeli |
| 1871 | | | Grant | | Gladstone |
| 1873 | Mackenzie | Dufferin | | | |
| 1875 | | | | | Disraeli |
| 1877 | | | Hayes | | |
| 1879 | Macdonald | Lorne | | | |
| 1881 | | | Garfield | | Gladstone |
| 1883 | | | Arthur | | |
| 1885 | | Lansdowne | Cleveland | | Marquess of Salisbury |
| 1887 | | | | | Gladstone |
| 1889 | | Preston | Harrison | | Marquess of Salisbury |
| 1891 | Abbott | | | | |
| 1893 | Thompson | Aberdeen | Cleveland | | Earl of Rosebery |
| 1895 | Bowell | | | | |
| 1897 | Tupper | | McKinley | | Marquess of Salisbury |
| 1899 | Laurier | Minto | | | |
| 1901 | | | | | |
| 1903 | | | Roosevelt | Edward VII | |
| 1905 | | Grey | | | Balfour |
| 1907 | | | | | Campbell-Bannerman |
| 1909 | | | | | Asquith |
| 1911 | Borden | Connaught | Taft | George V | |
| 1913 | | | Wilson | | |
| 1915 | | | | | |
| 1917 | | Devonshire | | | Lloyd-George |
| 1919 | | | | | |
| 1921 | Meighen | | | | |
| 1923 | King | Byng | Harding | | Law / Baldwin |
| 1925 | Meighen | | Coolidge | | MacDonald / Baldwin |

*Full names and titles of governors general appear on pp. 144-5.

# CANADA AND WORLD LEADERS (CONTINUED)

| YEAR | PRIME MINISTER | GOVERNOR GENERAL | U.S. PRESIDENT | MONARCH | U.K. PRIME MINISTER |
|---|---|---|---|---|---|
| 1927 | King | Ratton | Coolidge | George V | Baldwin |
| 1929 |  |  | Hoover |  | MacDonald |
| 1931 | Bennett |  |  |  |  |
| 1933 |  | Bessborough | Roosevelt |  |  |
| 1935 |  |  |  |  |  |
| 1937 | King | Tweedsmuir |  | Edward VIII | Baldwin |
| 1939 |  |  |  | George VI | Chamberlain |
| 1941 |  | Athlone |  |  | Churchill |
| 1943 |  |  |  |  |  |
| 1945 |  | Alexander | Truman |  | Attlee |
| 1947 |  |  |  |  |  |
| 1949 | St. Laurent |  |  |  |  |
| 1951 |  |  |  |  | Churchill |
| 1953 |  | Massey |  | Elizabeth II |  |
| 1955 |  |  | Eisenhower |  |  |
| 1957 |  |  |  |  | Eden |
| 1959 | Diefenbaker |  |  |  | Macmillan |
| 1961 |  | Vanier |  |  |  |
| 1963 |  |  | Kennedy |  | Douglas-Home |
| 1965 | Pearson |  | Johnson |  | Wilson |
| 1967 |  |  |  |  |  |
| 1969 | Trudeau | Michener |  |  |  |
| 1971 |  |  | Nixon |  | Heath |
| 1973 |  |  |  |  |  |
| 1975 |  | Leger | Ford |  | Wilson |
| 1977 |  |  |  |  | Callaghan |
| 1979 |  |  | Carter |  |  |
| 1981 | Clark / Trudeau | Schreyer |  |  | Thatcher |
| 1983 |  | Sauvé | Reagan |  |  |

# EIGHT

# Dates of Note

No book of political facts is complete without noting other events which transpired between the years 1867 and 1984. Many of these facts helped shape the outcome of our federal and provincial elections.

1867     **(July 1)-Prime Minister Sir John Alexander Macdonald takes office.**

(July 1)-Confederation-Ontario, Québec, New Brunswick, and Nova Scotia united to form Dominion of Canada.

(Nov. 6)-First session of Parliament opens.

1868     (April 7)-Assassination of D'arcy McGee, member of Parliament.

(July 1)-Northwest Territory acquired by Ruperts Land Act.

1870     (July 15)-Manitoba joins Canada as fifth province.

1871     (April 14)-Uniform monetary system established throughout Canada.

(July 20)-British Columbia becomes sixth province.

-First Canadian census-3,668,257.

1873     (April 2)-Pacific scandal revealed.

(May 20)-Royal Northwest Mounted Police established.

(July 1)-Prince Edward Island joins Canada as seventh province.

(Sept. 23)-First Canadian labour union formed.

**(Nov. 7)-Prime Minister Alexander Mackenzie takes office.**

1876     (June 5)-First session of Canadian Supreme Court held.

(July 3)-Intercolonial railway from Halifax to Québec opens.

(Aug. 10)-Alexander Graham Bell completes first long distance telephone call between Brantford and Paris, Ont. (8 miles or 12.8 km).

1877    (Jan. 13)-Fire destroys large section of Saint John, N.B.

1878    (June 20)-Australian or secret ballot first used.
**(Oct. 17)-Prime Minister Sir John Alexander Macdonald takes office.**

1881    Second Canadian census-4,324,810.

1882    Winnipeg becomes first Canadian community to have gas lighting.

1883    (Aug. 29)-First Salvation Army service in Canada at London, Ont.

(Nov. 18)-Standard time invented by Sandford Flemming, adopted by Canadian government.

1885    (Jan. 24)-Canadian Pacific Railway Telegraph from Atlantic to Pacific finished.
(Nov. 16)-Louis Riel, leader of Northwest Rebellion, hanged.

1886    (June 13)-Vancouver, B.C. destroyed by fire.

1887    (May 23)-First Canadian Pacific Railway train ride between Montréal, Québec and Vancouver, B.C. completed.

1888    (Mar. 1)-Parcel post service established between United States and Canada.

1891    Third Canadian census-4,883,239.
(June 6)-Death of Sir John Alexander Macdonald.
**(June 16)-Prime Minister Sir John Joseph Caldwell Abbott takes office.**

1892    (Feb. 23)-Lord Stanley, governor general of Canada, donates hockey trophy (Stanley Cup).

**(Dec. 5)-Prime Minister Sir John Sparrow David Thompson takes office.**

1894 (Sept. 3)-First Labour Day celebrated.
**(Dec. 21)-Prime Minister Sir Mackenzie Bowell takes office.**

1896 (Jan. 7)-Resignation of seven cabinet ministers under Prime Minister Sir Mackenzie Bowell.
**(May 1)-Prime Minister Sir Charles Hibbert Tupper, Bart. takes office.**
**(July 11)-Prime Minister Sir Wilfrid Laurier takes office.**

1898 (Feb. 18)-Klondike gold rush begins.

1899 (Oct. 29)-Canadian troops sent to South Africa to fight in Boer War.

1901 (Jan. 22)-Queen Victoria dies.
(April 1)-Canadian Census-5,371,315.
(Dec. 11)-Marconi receives first trans-Atlantic wireless message at St. John's, Newfoundland.

1903 (Jan. 24)-Alaska Boundary Treaty signed.

1905 (Sept. 1)-Alberta and Saskatchewan join Confederation.

1906 (Feb. 23)-Tommy Burns of Vancouver becomes first and only Canadian to win world heavyweight boxing championship.

1908 (Dec. 29)-Royal Mint opened in Ottawa.

1909 (Feb. 23)-First airplane flight in British Commonwealth by J.A.D. McCurdy at Baddeck, Nova Scotia.

(June 1)-Lord Grey donates top football prize (Grey Cup).

1910    (May 6)-Edward VII dies.

1911    **(Oct. 10)-Prime Minister Sir Robert Laird Borden takes office.**

1914    (Aug. 4)-Canada declares war on Germany (beginning of World War I).

1915    (Jan. 15)-Canadian National Railway line completed from Québec to Vancouver.

1916    (Feb. 3)-Federal Parliament buildings destroyed by fire.

(Mar. 13)-Manitoba first province to vote for Prohibition.

1917    (Jan. 18)-Federal income tax introduced.

(Feb. 12)-Sir Robert Borden first Canadian prime minister to attend a British cabinet meeting.

(April 10)-Canadian soldiers capture Vimy Ridge in France.

(Dec. 6)-Two ships collide in Halifax Harbour. Explosion kills 1,630 people.

(Dec. 17)-Women vote in federal elections for the first time.

1918    (April 2)-Famous German War Ace, Baron Von Richthofen (The Red Baron), shot down by Canadian pilot, Capt. Roy Brown.

(Nov. 11)-Armistice signed, bringing an end to World War I.

1919    (Mar. 3)-First international air mail service established between Vancouver and Seattle, Washington.

(May 15)-Winnipeg general strike begins.

(June 14)-First flight across Atlantic by Alcock and Brown.

1920     (Jan. 20)-Canada joins League of Nations as founding member.

(Feb. 1)-Royal Northwest Mounted Police becomes Royal Canadian Mounted Police.

**(July 11)-Prime Minister Arthur Meighen takes office.**

1921     (Dec. 6)-Agnes MacPhail becomes first woman elected to House of Commons.

**(Dec. 29)-Prime Minister William Lyon Mackenzie King takes office.**

1922     (Oct. 20)-Bonar Law of Rexton, N.B. becomes first British prime minister born outside of Britain.

1923     (July 26)-United States President Warren Harding becomes first U.S. president to visit Canada while in office.

(Dec. 10)-Dr. Frederick Banting wins Nobel Prize for medicine for his discovery of insulin.

1924     (April 1)-Royal Canadian Air Force founded.

1926     **(June 28)-Prime Minister Arthur Meighen takes office.**

**(Sept. 25)-Prime Minister William Lyon Mackenzie King takes office.**

1927     (July 1)-Canada celebrates its fiftieth anniversary (Diamond Jubilee).

1928     (Sept. 21)-First Canadian air mail stamps used.

1929    (Oct. 24)-Stock market crash.

1930    Cairine Wilson becomes first woman appointed to Senate.

**(Aug. 7)-Prime Minister Richard Bedford Bennett takes office.**

1931    (Feb. 12)-Statute of Westminster gives Canadian Parliament equality with British Parliament.

1934    (May 28)-Dionne quintuplets born in North Bay, Ontario.

1935    **(Oct. 23)-Prime Minister William Lyon Mackenzie King takes office.**

1936    (Jan. 20)-King George V of England dies, succeeded by Edward VIII, who renounces crown Dec. 10 and is succeeded by George VI.
(Nov. 2)-Canadian Broadcasting Corporation (CBC) created.

1937    (Oct. 17)-Trans Canada Airlines (TCA) established.

1939    (May 17)-Royal visit of King George VI and Queen Elizabeth.
(Sept. 1)-Germany attacks Poland, beginning World War II.
(Sept. 10)-Canada declares war on Germany.

1941    Two thousand Canadian soldiers killed or captured when Hong Kong falls to Japanese.

1942    National selective service for home service.
Beginning of rationing (sugar).
3,367 Canadian casualties at Dieppe, France.

| 1943 | First trans-Atlantic flight (TCA). |
| | (Aug. 11)-Québec City Conference between Churchill, Roosevelt, and Prime Minister King. |
| 1944 | (Sept. 11)-Second Québec Conference. |
| 1945 | (May 6)-V.E. Day |
| | (June 26)-United Nations Charter signed in San Francisco. |
| | (Sept. 2)-V.J. Day. |
| | (Oct. 24)-Canada joins United Nations. |
| 1947 | (Jan. 1)-Canadian Citizenship Act put into effect. |
| | (Sept. 20)-Canada elected to Security Council for two-year term. |
| 1948 | (Feb.)-Barbara Ann Scott wins ladies' world figure skating championship. |
| | **(Nov. 15)-Prime Minister Louis Stephen St. Laurent takes office.** |
| 1949 | (Feb. 18)-North Atlantic Treaty Organization (NATO) formed. |
| | (Mar. 31)-Newfoundland joins Canada as tenth province. |
| 1950 | (June 27)-Beginning of Korean War. |
| | (June 30)-Eskimos given right to vote. |
| 1951 | (July 13)-Shakespearean Festival opens at Stratford, Ontario. |
| | (Sept. 17)-First federal election held in Northwest Territories. |
| | (Oct. 8)-Princess Elizabeth and Prince Philip tour Canada. |
| 1952 | (Jan. 1)-Old age security begins. |

(Feb. 6)-King George VI dies.

(Feb. 28)-Vincent Massey becomes first Canadian-born governor general.

(Sept. 6)-First television broadcast from Montréal.

(Oct. 14)-Lester Pearson elected president of the United Nations General Assembly.

1953 (June 2)-Elizabeth II crowned Queen of England.

1954 (Jan. 8)-World's largest pipeline opens (Alberta to Ontario).

(Mar. 23)-First Canadian subway opens in Toronto.

1955 (Jan. 7)-Opening session of Parliament televised for first time.

1956 (Nov. 5)-Canada's Major General Burns made commander of U.N. International Force.

(Nov. 13)-Canada Council formed.

1957 **(June 21)-Prime Minister John George Diefenbaker takes office.**

(July 31)-D.E.W. (Distant Early Warning) line goes into operation.

(Oct. 14)-Lester Pearson receives Nobel Peace Prize.

(Nov. 3)-One of first atomic reactors opened at Chalk River, Ont.

1958 Blanche Meagher becomes first Canadian woman to hold ambassadorship (Israel).

(Oct. 23)-Springhill, Nova Scotia mine disaster claims lives of seventy-four miners.

1959 Queen Elizabeth and Prince Philip tour Canada.

(June 26)-St. Laurence Seaway officially opened.

1960    (Feb. 17)-Anne Heggtveit becomes first Canadian to win Olympic Gold Medal in skiing.
(July 1)-Indians on reservations given right to vote.
(Aug. 10)-Bill of Rights passed by Parliament.

1961    (May 16)-President Kennedy pays a state visit to Ottawa.

1962    (Jan. 16)-Gas pipeline explosion in Alberta.
(July 1)-Medicare comes into effect in Saskatchewan.
(Sept. 3)-Trans-Canada Highway officially opened at Rogers Pass, Alberta.
(Sept. 29)-First Canadian spacecraft "Alouette" is launched.

1963    **(April 22)-Prime Minister Lester Bowles Pearson takes office.**
(Sept. 16)-Largest wheat sale in history between Canada and Russia ($500 million).

1964    (May 2)-Northern Dancer becomes first Canadian horse to win Kentucky Derby.

1965    (Feb. 15)-New Canadian flag flown for first time.
(Nov. 9)-Power failure at Niagara Falls causes blackout of part of Ontario and Northeastern U.S.

1967    (Jan. 1)-Canada celebrates one hundredth anniversary of Confederation.
(April 18)-Expo 67 opens in Montréal.

1968    **(April 20)-Prime Minister Pierre Elliott Trudeau takes office.**

1970    (June 26)-Voting age reduced to eighteen.
(Oct. 13)-Canada recognizes communist China.

(Oct. 16)-War Measures Act put into effect after kidnapping, by the Front de Libération Québécois (FLQ), of Pierre LaPorte, Québec minister of labour and immigration, and James Cross, British trade commissioner.

1971    Gary Cowens of Kitchener, Ontario wins U.S. amateur golf championship.

1972    (Sept. 28)-Team Canada defeats Russia in first world hockey meeting.

1973    (May 29)-Ban on capital punishment except in special cases.
(Aug. 30)-One hundredth anniversary of RCMP.

1974    (Jan. 17)-First woman, Pauline McGibbon, appointed lieutenant governor of Ontario.
(April 30)-First Indian, Ralph Steinhauer, appointed lieutenant governor of Alberta.

1975    (Oct. 23)-First senator, Paul Lucier, chosen from northern Canada.

1976    (Feb. 22)-Sylvia Burka first Canadian to win world speed skating championship.
(July 17)-Olympic Games open in Montréal.

1977    (April 5)-Willie Adams becomes first Eskimo senator from Northwest Territories.

1979    (April 25)-Manitoba appeals court over-turned laws that prohibited use of French language in provincial Legislature, courts, and schools.
**(June 4)-Prime Minister Charles Joseph Clark takes office.**

| 1980 | **(March 3)-Prime Minister Pierre Elliott Trudeau takes office.** |
|------|------------------------------------------------------------------|
| 1981 | (April 23)-House of Commons approves final draft of new constitution<br>(Sept. 28)-Supreme Court rules on constitution. |
| 1982 | (April 17)-Queen Elizabeth II signs constitution<br>(May 2)-Bertha Wilson becomes first woman justice of Supreme Court of Canada.<br>(May 10)-Federal election campaign cut from sixty to fifty days. |
| 1983 | (June 11)-Brian Mulroney defeats Joe Clark in Conservative leadership race. |
| 1984 | (Feb.)-Gaêtan Boucher, speed skater, becomes first Canadian to win 3 Olympic medals (2 gold, 1 silver).<br>Jeanne Sauvé appointed first woman governor general. |

# Glossary

To understand our political system it is important to comprehend the idioms and jargon of the species. It is hoped that this section will aid the reader in that process.

**Acclamation**-Winning an election without opposition.

**Annex**-To add territory to an existing country.

**Assemblée Legislative**-Formerly (1965) Lower House of Québec Legislature.

**Assemblée Nationale**-Québec Legislature consisting of single House.

**Bennett buggy**-Automobile whose owner could no longer afford gas to run it; named after Depression Prime Minister R.B. Bennett.

**Bill 22**-Bill passed in 1974 by Québec Legislature designating French as only official language.

**Black Friday**-Date (June 1, 1956) Liberals used closure during pipeline debate in House of Commons.

**B.N.A. Act** (British North America Act, 1867)-Act passed by British Parliament uniting provinces of Québec, Ontario, New Brunswick, and Nova Scotia into the Dominion of Canada; renamed Constitution Act, 1867.

**Cabinet**-Elected members of governing party chosen by prime minister to head various departments of government.

**Canadian Bill of Rights**-Legislation which guarantees right and freedoms of citizens, passed in 1960 under prime ministership of John Diefenbaker.

**CCF** (Co-operative Commonwealth Federation)-Political party formed in 1932 under first leadership of J.S. Woodsworth; later (1961) renamed New Democratic Party.

**Charlottetown Conference**-First official meeting held by Fathers of Confederation regarding union of British North America.

**Closure**-A cabinet minister's motion to shorten bill in House of Commons.

**Commons**-Lower House of federal government to which members must be elected.

**Confederation**-Uniting of Ontario, Québec, New Brunswick, and Nova Scotia in 1867 into federal union under B.N.A. Act.

**Conservative party**-One of Canada's two first federal political parties, which, over the years, has also been known as the Liberal-Conservative and Progressive Conservative party; Sir John A. Macdonald was first Conservative prime minister.

**Créditistes**-Québec branch of Social Credit party.

**Dominion**-Self-governing nation of the British Commonwealth.

**Electoral district**-An area of qualified voters.

**Fathers of Confederation**-Delegates of Charlottetown, Québec and London Conferences resulting in 1867 Confederation.

**Federal Parliament or government**-Consists of House of Commons and Senate.

**Gerrymander**-A redistricting of constituency boundaries usually to the advantage of one party.

**Government House**-Governor general's (Rideau Hall) or lieutenant governor's official residence.

**Governor general**-Official representative of sovereign in Canada; until 1952 a British citizen; Vincent Massey was the first Canadian governor general.

**Green chamber**-Main chamber of the House of Commons.

**Grit**-Early name for Liberal party (as in men of true grit).

**Hansard**-Official record of debates of House of Commons.

**House of Commons**-See Commons.

**Incumbent**-Present office holder.

**Legislative Assembly**-Governing provincial body consisting of elected members (M.L.A.s).

**Liberal party**-One of Canada's two first federal political parties; Alexander Mackenzie was the first Liberal prime minister.

**Lieutenant governor**-Representative of sovereign in the provinces.

**Majority government**-Party having more than half of the seats in federal House of Commons or provincial Legislature.

**Maple Leaf**-National emblem of Canada.

**Minority government**-Party having less than half of the seats in the federal House of Commons or provincial Legislature.

**M.L.A.**-Member of Legislative Assembly.

**Money bill**-Bill dealing with financial matters; must be recommended by governor general and originate in the House of Commons.

**M.P.**-Member of Parliament.

**NDP**-New Democratic Party; first leader was T.C. Douglas (1961); see also CCF.

**Opposition**-Party having second largest number of seats in House of Commons or provincial legislature; also known as official opposition headed by leader of opposition.

**Parti Québécois**-Québec provincial party formed in 1968 with René Lévesque as first leader and objective of making Québec into a single independent state.

**Parti Rouge**-Political party founded by L.J. Papineau; later to become Québec branch of Liberal party.

**Premier**-Chief executive of provincial party in power.

**Prime minister**-Chief executive of federal party in power.

**Progressive party**-Political party formed in 1920, primarily a western farmers party; first leader was T.R. Crerar.

**Public bill**-A bill of general nature introduced in either the House of Commons or Senate.

**Red chamber**-Main chamber of the Senate.

**Riding**-electoral district.

**Royal assent**-Signing of legislation by monarch or representative; final stage in the passing of a bill.

**Seat**-Electoral district.

**Senator**-Member of the upper House appointed by the prime minister.

**Separatism**-Province separating itself from the rest of Canada and forming an individual state.

**Social Credit**-Political party formed in 1930s.

**Speaker**-Presiding officer of House of Commons and Senate.

**Statute of Westminster** (1931)-Act making Canada autonomous.

**Tory**-A member of the Conservative party.

**Union Nationale**-Québec provincial party; first leader was Paul Gouin; however, party was dominated by Maurice Duplessis.

**Whig**-Another name for a member of Liberal party; rarely used today except in the U.K.

# Bibliography

The books listed here are by no means all the books on the subject but, rather, a select list to aid the reader who wishes to further his or her research.

Allen, Ralph. *Ordeal by Fire*. Toronto: Doubleday Canada Ltd., 1961.

Beck, J. Murray. *Pendulum of Power, Canada's Federal Elections*. Scarborough: Prentice-Hall Canada Inc., 1968.

Bowman, Bob. *Dateline: Canada*. Toronto: Holt, Rinehart and Winston of Canada Ltd., 1973.

Campbell, Colin. *Canadian Political Facts: 1945-1976*. Toronto: Methuen Publications, 1977.

Colombo, John Robert (ed.). *Colombo's Canadian Quotations*. Edmonton: Hurtig Publishers Ltd., 1974.

Cook, Ramsay. *Canada, A Modern Study*. Toronto: Clarke, Irwin and Co. Ltd., 1977.

Courtney, John C. *The Selection of National Party Leaders in Canada*. Toronto: Macmillan of Canada, 1973.

Creighton, Donald. *Dominion of the North*. Toronto: Macmillan of Canada, 1957.

Creighton, Donald. *John A. Macdonald*. 2 vols. Toronto: Macmillan of Canada, 1956.

DaForte, J.W. *Laurier, A Study in Canadian Politics*. Toronto: McClelland and Stewart Ltd., 1963.

Donaldson, Gordon. *Sixteen Men: Canada's Prime Ministers*. Toronto: Doubleday Canada Ltd., 1980.

Hamilton, Robert M. and Shields, Dorothy. *The Dictionary of Canadian Quotations and Phrases*. Toronto: McClelland and Stewart Ltd., 1982.

Hardy, W.G. *From Sea Unto Sea*. Garden City, New York: Doubleday and Co., 1980.

Hutchison, Bruce. *The Incredible Canadian*. Don Mills: Longman Canada Ltd., 1952.

Hutchison, Bruce. *Mr. Prime Minister, 1867-1964*. Don Mills: Longman Canada Ltd., 1964.

Kerr, D.G.G. *Historical Atlas of Canada*. 3rd rev. ed. Don Mills: Thomas Nelson and Sons (Canada), 1975.

Millgate, Linda. *The Almanac of Dates*. New York: Harcourt Brace Jovanovich, 1977.

Newman, Peter C. *Renegade in Power*. Toronto: McClelland and Stewart Ltd., 1963.

Normandin, Pierre G. (ed.). *Canadian Parliamentary Guide, 1970-1983*. Ottawa: Pierre G. Normandin, 1970-1983.

Pearson, Lester B. *Mike: The Memoirs of the Right Honourable Lester B. Pearson*. 3 vols. Toronto: University of Toronto Press, 1972-75.

Schull, Joseph. *The Nation Makers*. Toronto: Macmillan of Canada, 1967.